IT'S ABOUT SKIING AND NOT THE SKIS

IT'S ABOUT SKIING AND NOT THE SKIS

Behavior Theory, Skiing, and Ski Teaching

JAY EACKER

iUniverse, Inc.
Bloomington

It's About Skiing and Not the Skis
Behavior Theory, Skiing, and Ski Teaching

iUniverse books may be ordered through booksellers or by contacting:

iUniverse
1663 Liberty Drive
Bloomington, IN 47403
www.iuniverse.com
1-800-Authors (1-800-288-4677)

ISBN: 978-1-4502-6787-8 (sc)
ISBN: 978-1-4502-6788-5 (dj)
ISBN: 978-1-4502-6789-2 (ebk)

Library of Congress Control Number: 2010916059

Printed in the United States of America

iUniverse rev. date: 10/27/2010

Table of Contents

I

Preface

Several years ago, Lance Armstrong and his ghostwriter, Sally Jenkins, wrote a book entitled "It's Not About the Bike". They were right. It wasn't about the bike. It was about what we do with a bike, or, biking. More precisely, it was about bicycling and how it brought Lance back to life after his bout with cancer. Whether biking, bicycling, or coming back to life, we are doing something, or, behaving.

The same can be said about any other thing that we do and especially sports. For example, tennis is not about the racquet. It is about hitting a tennis ball or playing tennis. Similarly, rowing is not about the oars and the boat, but about making the boat move. Running is not about the shoes, but what we do with the shoes. Fishing is not about the fish. And, skiing is not about the skis. In all instances, it is about what we do when we do them, or, our behavior. What follows is a more in depth analysis of what is going on when we are doing something and, in particular, skiing.

II

Introduction

Some time ago, I was talking about skiing with a long time, long ago, professional ski instructor of America (PSIA) national demonstration team member who has spent most of his life skiing and not a little thinking about it. His name was Paul Jones otherwise known as "P J". More will be said about him later.

He pointed out that there was no theory of skiing let alone ski teaching. Well, skiing and ski teaching don't have to have a theory, but it would be nice if they did.

It would be nice because then skiers and ski instructors would have something to hang their hats, caps, or helmets on. That is, they would have some sense of what it was they were about and what they were trying to accomplish. From my perspective, behavior theory is ideally suited for that purpose.

However, there is at least one problem with theories. They sometimes sound like they are true and so may stifle further inquiry. Truth, in turn, has its own problems. One is knowing when something is true. So far as we can know, human inquiry is

3

never complete. It could go on forever or at least as long as there are humans who inquire. Consequently, even if we knew the truth (and it could set us free), we couldn't know that we knew it. With that caveat, I hereby offer the following as a theory of skiing and ski teaching behavior.

Stated somewhat differently, it was perfectly obvious to me then, as it is still obvious to me now, that skiing does have a theory. It's just that no one has taken the time to point out what it is. That's what I propose to do here. Demonstrate the obvious.

It's not too surprising that I would think the way I do about skiing. Up until my retirement from college teaching about seven years ago, I considered myself a behavior analyst in the tradition of John Watson, Clark Hull, and B. F. Skinner. Now, I am just an old guy who still likes to ski and who has spent a lot of time thinking about it.

III

Behavior Theory

Whatever else it may be, skiing is something that we do. It is a behavior. Indeed, the essence of skiing, if there is one, may be that it is simply something that we do with boards on our feet.

Some skiing is more effective, more efficient, more effortless, more elegant, more esthetic than other skiing. That's what makes it so endlessly fascinating. Some of us do it naturally. Others have to learn how. For that, we sometimes hire ski instructors.

Whatever else it may be, ski instructing or ski teaching is also something that we do. Indeed, the essence of ski teaching, if there is one, may be that it is simply something that we do to change skiing behavior. Some of it is more effective, more efficient, more effortless, more elegant, more esthetic than other ski teaching. That, too, makes it endlessly fascinating. Some of us do it naturally. Others have to learn how. For that, ski instructors hire clinicians.

Since skiing and ski teaching are both things that we do, we might expect that the same principles apply to both. Those principles are in effect when we ski as well as when we teach skiing, but they are not well known. Some of the major ones will be examined here. Collectively, they constitute a theory of skiing and ski teaching.

Principles of Behavior
Or
Principles of Skiing and Ski Teaching

There are a half dozen or so major principles of behavior that apply to skiing and ski teaching. They are based on an experimental analysis of behavior. Actually, there are many more than that but some of them are so obscure that only a behavior analyst could be interested in them. In addition, there are two major categories of behavior to which most of them apply and so, all told, there may be more than a dozen that help to explain skiing and ski teaching behavior.

The major categories of behavior are respondent behavior and operant behavior. Respondent behaviors are those elicited by stimuli in the environment such as those studied by Ivan Pavlov. Everyone knows about Pavlov and his dog. His interest was piqued by salivation but much of what he discovered applies to emotions and especially fear as well as, perhaps, excitement. Skiers as well as ski instructors know a lot about fear and excitement, or elation, first hand. More will be said about emotions as we go along.

Operant behaviors are those that have an effect on the environment. They "operate" on the environment and were studied extensively by B. F. Skinner. Among them are the edging, pressuring, and rotary movements that occur when we make a turn with our skis. They have an effect on the environment and, in turn, those effects affect what occurs next. More will also be said about them as we go along.

For the most part, the major principles of behavior apply to operants, but there are some that also apply to respondents. Those principles are: positive and negative reinforcement, response differentiation or shaping, punishment, extinction, generalization, discrimination, and schedules of reinforcement. Whoops! That makes eight. I miscounted. Actually, when you consider that there are eight schedules of reinforcement, the number increases still more.

Positive Reinforcement

Anything that increases the rate of some behavior is a positive reinforcer. It doesn't matter why it increases the behavior. It only matters that it does. A reinforcer is reinforcing because of its effects on behavior, not because of some property intrinsic to it. Thus, for example, simply making a turn with the skis may increase the rate of the behaviors that contributed to it. In addition, of course, a ski instructor saying "Good!" may work as well.

Response Differentiation
Or
Shaping

Behavior can be molded, or shaped, by reinforcing those that more and more closely approximate some final performance. Thus, for example, when a ski instructor says "Hey! That was pretty good, but now try to flex your knees a little more", she is using this principle. It is especially evident that the ski instructor is using the principle if she keeps raising the standard for praising her pupil until the student makes a perfect turn (which, of course, never happens so far as we know). Reinforcers may also occur naturally as when the skier makes the turn more efficiently, that is, with less effort or leaves parallel tracks in the snow.

Negative Reinforcement

While on the subject of effort, whenever some behavior reduces effort and increases in rate, we have a case of negative reinforcement. Thus, for example, when a skier stands more balanced over the skis and it reduces the strain on the back and thigh muscles, the behavior of balancing is negatively reinforced. Similarly, whenever we make a turn more efficiently, it reduces the difficulty of making the turn, and we are more likely to make the turn that way in the future. As a result, a behavior may be both positively and negatively reinforced at the same time. That is, if the turn reduces the difficulty in making it, it is negatively reinforced. And, if our tracks in the snow are more parallel to each other, it is positively reinforced provided, of course, that the rate of making that turn increases.

Punishment

Unfortunately, punishment is also effective in changing behavior and it, too, may occur along with negative and positive reinforcement. Thus, for example, when a skier "leans back" he may feel the strain on his thigh muscles. If "leaning back" then decreases in rate, we have a case of punishment.

Now, when he straightens up, or becomes more balanced over the skis, and balancing increases in rate, we have a case of negative reinforcement. And, when he is then more comfortable on his skis and comfort increases in rate, we have a case of positive reinforcement.

Punishment decreases the rate of some response when that response produces it. Negative reinforcement increases the rate of some response when that response removes it. And, positive reinforcement increases the rate of some response when that response produces it.

With all three principles occurring at, or about, the same time you would think that "leaning back" or being out of balance on the skis would get eliminated pretty quickly. As most experienced ski instructors know, it doesn't. There are probably other well established behaviors that interfere with it. They may be emotion or fear which are also things that we do. More will be said about them later.

Extinction

When a previously reinforced behavior is no longer reinforced, it decreases in rate or extinguishes. However, the rate may not return to zero. There may be a lingering residual for the effects of reinforcement and that may be a part of why it takes so long to eliminate some behavior. In addition, of course, some features of the old behavior may still get reinforced and interfere with the new.

Thus, for example, when a ski instructor gets a student to turn on her outside ski, and it becomes a pretty good turn, it may take a while for that student to become more two-footed. One-footed turns may still get reinforced by their naturally occurring consequences even though the instructor may no longer encourage them or the new, shaped, skis no longer reinforce them.

Schedules of Reinforcement

How quickly a behavior extinguishes depends, in part at least, on the previous schedule of reinforcement. Schedules have to do with the way in which reinforcement occurs or is administered. For example, reinforcement can occur after every response or after every other response. In addition, it can occur after every fifth response or, on the average, after every fifth response. In fact, the schedule can be ratio or interval, fixed or variable, and simple or complex. Their combinations give rise to at least eight different ways in which reinforcement occurs or can be administered.

Actually, there are many more schedules than that but only behavior analysts could possibly be interested in them. For example, B. F. Skinner wrote an entire book entitled simply *Schedules of Reinforcement.*

Complex schedules are made up of the simple ones, but none of the complex schedules may occur in the natural environment even though behavior analysts can arrange conditions in a behavior laboratory to study them. Nevertheless, if each constitutes a separate principle of behavior, then all told there are more than two dozen principles of behavior that help to explain it.

A simple schedule of reinforcement is illustrated by a ski instructor saying "Good!" after every thing that a beginning student does. In this case, there is a fixed ratio of responses to reinforcement. It is continuous or a fixed ratio of one, one response for one reinforcement. Behaviors get established very quickly on this schedule of reinforcement. Unfortunately, they also extinguish very quickly.

When the ratio of responses to reinforcement is increased, we have still another fixed ratio schedule of reinforcement and so on for fixed ratios that can become quite large. Early on in teaching skiing, the instructor may use a continuous schedule of praise for her student's efforts because, as said, it quickly establishes the behavior in which she is interested if only just walking around on the skis.

Later in the lesson, she may shift to a variable ratio schedule of responses to reinforcement where, on the average, every other response is reinforced. Variable ratio schedules establish rather high rates of responses over long periods of time that are quite resistant to extinction. They are the ones most commonly encountered in the natural environment which may help to explain why some skiing behaviors are so persistent.

For example, bending at the waist can get established early and take a long time to extinguish. Some of us know that from personal experience and may do it longer than we care to admit.

The reinforcer for it is probably balance, and it may persist until fore and aft, side to side, balancing get established and interfere with it. Then, bending at the waist is no longer reinforced and extinguishes.

The two remaining simple schedules of reinforcement are based on the time interval since the last reinforced response. Thus, for example, if the time interval since the last reinforced response is one minute, the schedule is a fixed interval one minute. If the time interval since the last reinforced response varies around some average value, the schedule is a variable interval schedule of reinforcement. Since ski instructors and clinicians seldom if ever time the intervals between reinforced responses with a stopwatch, these schedules seldom if ever occur in ski teaching.

Generalization

Fortunately, a behavior established under one set of circumstances occurs under other similar circumstances. That is, behavior generalizes. Thus, once we get a student walking around with skis on flat terrain, it is easier to get them walking around in skis on terrain that is not quite so flat. That is fortunate because we then don't have to teach walking around with skis all over again under those changed circumstances.

Discrimination

Fortunately, a behavior established under one set of circumstances doesn't occur under all other circumstances. That is, discrimination occurs, but it must be taught or shaped by way of differential reinforcement and extinction. All that means is that the ski instructor reinforces the behavior under one set of circumstances but doesn't reinforce it under others. Thus, he may praise a student for getting her boots on the right feet but not when she doesn't. In addition, of course, the student may be punished by boots on the wrong feet so discrimination training is not simply a matter of differential reinforcement and extinction. It may also include punishment as well as extinction.

Operant Conditioning

Up to now, most of what has been related here has been about operant conditioning. Simply stated, the principle of operant conditioning is that operants are change by their consequences. Some of those consequences are positive and negative reinforcement, punishment, and extinction.

Operant behaviors are widespread in skiing. They include all of those behaviors that help us to get around in the skiing environment. As a result, they include skiing itself but also getting on a chair lift. Getting on a chair lift changes our view of the mountain we are skiing and so may be reinforced by that view, and it can also be exciting if not downright scary when we do it for the first time. That is where respondent conditioning comes in.

Respondent Conditioning

The principle of respondent conditioning is that respondents are changed when their normal stimuli are paired with others as in the case of Pavlov's dog. As stated earlier, respondents are evoked, like a reflex, by what's going on in the environment. That principle was perhaps the first demonstration by anyone that behavior is lawful and orderly.

When we ski, all kinds of things in the skiing environment can evoke, or elicit, respondents. They can vary all the way from excitement, to wonder, to fear, to elation, to exuberance, to joy. You name it. All kinds of feelings can be produced. For behavior analysts, feelings are also things that we do. They are behaviors. When the stimuli that bring out those emotions are paired with other stimuli in the skiing environment, they too come to evoke those emotions just as salivation was produced by the metronome, or bell, in Pavlov's demonstration.

Obviously, behavior analysts treat emotions as behavior. However, they occur inside of us. They are covert rather than overt as in the case of, for example, making a ski turn. But, they can interfere with making a ski turn as well as, on occasion, enhancing it.

If we are timid about making a ski turn and timidity is a covert behavior, it can interfere with making the turn properly. On the other hand, being too bold about making the turn and being bold is a covert behavior can also interfere with making the turn properly. There are, of course, all shades of emotion between timidity and boldness. We need the right balance, neither too timid nor too bold, to make the turn properly.

In addition, of course, fear or the lack of it may also be involved. Fortunately, it too can be dealt with as a covert behavior by way of behavior principles. One is respondent extinction.

Respondent Extinction

The principle of respondent extinction is that repeated presentations of the new stimulus in the absence of the one that normally elicits the respondent reduces the strength of the conditioned respondent. Thus, for example, if the chair lift evokes a fear response, repeatedly exposing the student to the moving chair without asking them to sit in it may help to reduce the fear of a moving chair. In addition, repeatedly sitting in a stationary chair may help to reduce the fear of a moving chair.

Similarly, getting on and off a slow moving chair may help to eliminate the fear of a faster moving chair. And, of course, simply getting on an off a faster moving chair may help to eliminate or reduce the fear of a still faster moving chair. There are all kinds of ways to use this principle and the one that works is the right one for a particular student. When it works, it reinforces the operant behavior of the ski instructor who implemented that procedure whatever it was.

To give another example, the word "lemon" in this sentence may evoke salivation by some of you as you are reading this sentence right now. If it does, the behavior of salivation is explained by the fact that the word "lemon" has been paired with real lemons on several occasions in your past, or, respondent conditioning. Now, when the word "lemon" occurs in this sentence at this moment, it evokes salivation right now just as real lemons have evoked it in your past. If it doesn't, the respondent conditioning procedure may not have been as extensive for you as it has for others or else the behavior of salivation may have undergone respondent extinction.

The principle of respondent conditioning explains your salivation to the word "lemon" on this page right now. The principle of respondent extinction explains your no longer doing so after the word "lemon" has occurred several times on this page but is no longer paired with a real lemon. Since fear is a respondent just as salivation is a respondent, or, they are evoked by the environment, both are explained by the principles of respondent conditioning and by respondent extinction. Those two principles have far reaching effects on skiing and ski teaching behavior.

Two Anomalies

There are at least two additional principles of behavior that enter in to behavior theory but that don't seem to fit in to it as well as those that have been mentioned so far. From that standpoint, they are anomalies where an anomaly is something that is out of keeping with the natural order of things. One is imitation. The other is superstition.

Imitation

People, and other organisms, do what other people, and other organisms, do. That's the principle. Try walking down a crowded street looking up at the sky. Others will do the same. Not all of them, but a good many. It has been demonstrated between people, between other organisms, and between people and other organisms. It may ultimately be shown to be a matter of the more basic principles, most notably reinforcement, discrimination, and generalization, but for now may be taken for a basic principle in its own right.

Certainly, ski instructors are well acquainted with it not only in their own skiing but also in their ski teaching. We try to imitate the skiing behavior of those we consider to be good skiers, and our students try to imitate us. In fact, we rely on it whenever we give a demonstration of what we would have our students do.

Superstition.

The second principle, superstition, refers to any instance where a behavior occurs along with a reinforcing consequence but they are independent of each other. In other words, there is a correlation between the response and reinforcement but no contingency. Thus, when an exaggerated hip movement occurs along with a pretty good turn on the skis, the exaggerated hip movement may increase in rate along with all of the other movements that contribute to the turn.

Similarly, when ski racers image a course just before they ski it, imaging behavior may increase in rate along with the successful completion of the course. To the extent that there is only a correlation between imaging and successful completion of the course, imaging is superstitious. And, of course, when we pray for snow and it snows, praying for snow behavior may also increase in rate.

Now, it may be true that praying behavior is superstitious but only to the extent that religious doctrines are false. However, since we cannot know whether religious doctrines are false, we cannot know whether praying behavior is superstitious. Nevertheless, there are those who would place it in that category just as there are those who would call rubbing a rabbit's foot just before a ski race for good luck superstitious or imaging the course superstitious.

However, superstitious behavior has a second characteristic. Not only is it merely correlated with reinforcement, but it also "drifts". That is, it may change over time. As a result, the exaggerated hip movement may change, not because of anything a ski instructor or the student may do, but simply because it doesn't contribute to the reinforcing consequence of the turn itself. It may be correlated with reinforcement but doesn't produce it. Knowing about this principle (where knowing is something that we do and a case of discrimination) my keep us alert to the contingency between skiing behavior and reinforcement as opposed to the correlation between skiing behavior and reinforcement.

A Note on the Nature-Nurture Controversy

Like it or not, these two anomalies raise the specter of the nature-nurture controversy. That controversy has to do with the respective contributions of natural athletic ability and environmental factors in accounting for skiing behavior.

Many years ago, B. F. Skinner wrote an article entitled *The Phylogeny and Ontogeny of Behavior.* I will spare you the details.

Suffice it to say that, in that article, he proposed that the phylogeny of behavior, the species origins of behavior, had to do with natural selection or evolution whereas the ontogeny of behavior, the behavior of an individual during its lifetime, had to do with learning and, in particular, operant conditioning.

Evolution or natural selection selects individuals particularly sensitive to the contingencies of reinforcement that occur in a particular environment whereas those contingencies select out the kinds of behaviors displayed by that individual in that environment during its lifetime. That, in brief, is the phylogeny and the ontogeny of behavior and how learning may fine tune evolution.

With regard to imitation, there appears to be a greater phylogenic, or evolutionary, component. It is not instinctive, that is another issue, but perhaps extremely sensitive to the reinforcers for it and so may occur early and often in the lifetime of the individual. It has survival value.

With regard to superstition, there appears to be a greater balance between the phylogeny of behavior and the ontogeny of behavior, but it may not be all that adaptive. Since all that is required is a correlation between the behavior and reinforcement, all kinds of bizarre behaviors may get shaped up and so may not have as much survival value for the individual. The jury is out on whether that applies to skiing behavior.

Discussion

More could be said about the ways in which behavior principles can be used to change skiing and ski teaching behavior. In fact, more will be said as we go along.

For now, it may suffice to note just a few other instances in which these principles enter in to and affect skiing behavior. For example, some students and many ski instructors have encountered, or experienced, the profound reinforcing consequences of skiing up to a more experienced ski instructor, clinician, or member of a regional or national demonstration team and having them say, in a quiet voice, "Nice turns!"

On the other hand, there is a relativity to reinforcement. A long time long ago member of the PSIA national demonstration team, P J, tells the story on himself about some young ski racers he was coaching who wrote "Nice turns, nice turns" on square after square of toilet paper and handed the roll to him when their ski camp was finished. Reinforcers aren't always reinforcing and, sometimes, when they are overused we can be told what to do with them.

Similarly, an experienced skier who has just skied a mogul run with some style and finesse can attest to the reinforcing consequences of just finishing the run. In addition, of course, intermediate and upper levels of skiers can vouch for the consequences of leaving "first tracks" on a run recently covered with fresh powdered snow. Finally, there is the beginning student of skiing who has just glided forward on her skis for the first time or made her first turn.

Why is a Reinforcer Reinforcing?

Those examples may raise, for some, the question of why a reinforcer is reinforcing. When asked that question some years ago, B. F. Skinner replied "Because of its effects on behavior". He was almost immediately criticized for the apparent circularity of that reply but, when you think about it (where thinking is also something that we do), it makes good sense.

Reinforcers are called reinforcers because of their effects on behavior and almost anything can be a reinforcer so long as it increases the rate of some behavior. In fact, it appears to be that efforts to answer that question lead to theories of reinforcement when it may be enough to simply identify them.

Indeed, the essence of reinforcement, if there is one, may not be intrinsic to it at all but, rather, that such a consequence allows us to do something else. For example, what may reinforce skiing behavior for all levels of skiers may simply be putting boards on their feet and then moving down a hill regardless of how fast they do it.

In addition, some of us may feel (where feeling is also something that we do) a rush of endorphins or adrenaline when we have finished a run or a day of skiing. Skiing (something that we do) allows us to feel the rush (something else that we do). Similarly, skiing a difficult run allows us to look back up the hill to see what we have accomplished (where seeing is also something that we do; it is a behavior). We couldn't look back up the hill to see what we had done if we hadn't skied that run. It really doesn't matter why a reinforcer is reinforcing so long as it has that effect and, in the long run (pardon the pun) that may be all there is to it in spite of all our theories of reinforcement to the contrary.

Why is a Punisher Punishing?

A similar argument might be developed about punishment. Ordinarily, we consider a punisher to be an aversive stimulus; one that we try to get away from. However, almost anything can punish a response if, when it is produced, the rate of that response decreases. Thus, for example, a ski instructor may use excessive praise to reinforce anything his student does but, if the rate of those responses decreases, may find that his praise is punishment rather than reinforcement. If the student's responses produce excessive praise and they then decrease in rate, they are being punished rather than reinforced.

Summary and Conclusion

To sum up, by way of their research and teaching, behavior analysts have developed laws and principles of behavior that can then be used to explain behavior; those principles can also be used to change behavior. Collectively, the laws and principles of behavior constitute a theory.

Some of those laws and principles include: respondent conditioning, operant conditioning, positive reinforcement, differentiation or shaping, negative reinforcement, punishment, extinction, generalization, discrimination, schedules of reinforcement, operant conditioning, respondent conditioning, respondent extinction, imitation, and superstition. Since skiing and ski teaching are behaviors or things that skiers do, those principles can be used to explain their behavior and to change it.

Overt and Covert Behavior

Most of the things that skiers do are overt; we can see them. However, some of the things that skiers do are covert; we can't see them. Nevertheless, behavior principles can be used to change them along with the overt behavior.

Covert behaviors include thinking and feeling as well as seeing and hearing. For behavior analysts, we don't do something because we have thought about it; we do something and (sometimes) have thought about it. Both the thinking and the doing require explanation by way of the laws and principles of behavior.

The same goes for emotions or how we feel. We don't ski down a hill because it makes us feel good (although that may be one of the reinforcing consequences), we ski down a hill and we may feel good (although not always). Both the skiing and the feeling good require explanation by way of the laws and principles of behavior, at least according to behavior analysts.

Conclusion

In conclusion, it isn't our inner behavior that explains our outer behavior. Rather, both the inner or covert behavior and the outer or overt behavior require explanation by way of laws and principles. They, in turn, can be used to change behavior and, in particular, that of skiers and those who teach it.

IV

Skiing

Control

Some instances from my own skiing history may help to illustrate how it has been shaped, or controlled, by its consequences. Control, of course, is a relative term. It doesn't mean, in this case, that behavior is coerced or forced or caused. It simply means that the consequences as well as perhaps the antecedents have affected it. The laws and principles of behavior, as with all scientific laws and principles, are always probable and never certain, probably.

The topic of control also raises the question of who, or what, controls. Many years ago, B. F. Skinner wrote a utopian novel called *Walden Two* in which he explored that question as well as the application of these principles in the design of a culture.

Simply stated, the question is "Who controls the controller"? The answer was not immediately obvious, but it soon became clear that, if we control the environment (at least to some extent) and it, in turn, controls us then we are both the controller and the controllee. Sometimes, the environment controls us and, sometimes, we control the environment. That is quite clearly the case when we ski.

The topic of control also provides a link between behavior theory and evolution. As everyone knows, the theory of evolution comes from the work of Charles Darwin. His theory emphasized the role of chance variation and natural selection in the origin of species. That is, our chromosomes and genes combine in various ways at random to produce individual members of a species. Then, those individual members of a species are selected out that are best adapted to prevailing conditions in the environment. When those conditions change, the species may change along with them. In this case, control is exerted primarily by the environment.

In behavior theory, it is behavior that is controlled or selected by prevailing conditions in the environment. Not all environments are equally reinforcing or punishing. Those conditions that prevail select the behaviors of the individual members of a species living under them, and they are not all equally affected which may help to account for individual differences. Sometimes, we are able to control those environmental conditions as when we build a house or find shelter and warmth in a cave. Sometimes, we don't and adapt or die out. Sometimes, we control and sometimes we are controlled. (There is a country western ballad that illustrates this point more precisely in the lyric that "sometimes we are the windshield and sometimes we are the bug").

From that standpoint, behavior theory suggests a way in which the individual is further adapted to its environment. If behavior theory is about learning, then learning may fine tune evolution.

Beginnings

My first serious introduction to skiing took place some thirty years ago when a friend and colleague, Professor Steve Rubin, casually mentioned

"I just bought a new pair of ski boots".

"Oh? What's so special about that?"

"They only cost a little over two hundred dollars".

"Was that a bargain?"

"To me it was".

"Why"?

"I like to ski".

"What's to like about skiing"?

"It's fun. It's exciting. It's exercise. It's a challenge. It's out of doors. It's fun. It's exciting. It's exercise. It's a challenge. It's out of doors".

"You're repeating yourself".

"I know. Skiing's like that. It's all of those things and more".

"Oh, really"?

"Yes, really. You'll have to find out for yourself".

"Well, maybe someday, I will".

That sort of ended our conversation at that time, but it did get me started thinking about skiing. Thinking, of course, is something that we do and that is also affected by its consequences.

One thought was that it was a lot to spend on a some time winter sport and that he must have been out of his mind. Little did I know.

Prior to that conversation with Steve, I had tried to ski as a kid with a borrowed pair of wooden skis and leather loops for whatever boots I was wearing. The results were disastrous. I spent most of an afternoon floundering around in the snow on the foothills near my home town of Weiser, Idaho and didn't try again until I was in college. Floundering around in the snow is not likely to increase the rate of skiing behavior, and it didn't.

Later, in college, I "went skiing" with a girl friend near her home in Coeur d'Alene, Idaho I think it was. She gave me a few perfunctory tips about standing up on the skis, pointed me toward a rope tow, and skied off with the rest of her family. Needless to say, I again floundered around for another afternoon, and my skiing behavior as well as our romance of course were soon at an end. It's a wonder I was willing to try it again after so much punishment.

At about the time my friend Steve made his comment about ski boots, I was a single parent with two pre-teenaged daughters, Anne and Jane; she later changed the spelling to Jayne. We were looking for a winter sport that would get us out of doors in the fresh air and away from the television set. We were also trying to get away from the memory of their mother who had died some months earlier. Skiing appeared to be the answer. That first season, we took a lesson each time we skied. One of our more experienced skiing friends had advised it. Not Steve, he sort of prides himself on never having taken a lesson, and it shows as I have told him many times.

First Lesson

We started at Brundage Mountain near Payette Lakes in McCall, Idaho. Some years later, I learned from the man himself that the mountain had been developed by Corey Engen, brother of Alf and Sverre Engen, and that he had also contributed to the development of the ski area at Anthony Lakes near La Grande, Oregon. At that time, I also took a semi-private lesson from him and, while he was clearly a very good skier, all I remember about the lesson was "Okay, now. Let's make the turn. Nice and easy!" just before he skied off to demonstrate.

But, I digress. Our first lesson was with a woman ski instructor at Brundage who must have known what she was doing because, by the end of it, we were all three making ragged wedge turns and using the rope tow. That, of course, was a vast improvement over my earlier experience in college and as a kid.

If not Anne and Jayne, I at least was near exhaustion by the end of the lesson. In fact, I later realized that, although near exhaustion, I was a bit euphoric, and the euphoria lasted for several days. We spent a lot of time sledding and hiking in the snow for the remainder of that trip and were ecstatic about just being outside and able to do it. But, I was also hooked by what we had accomplished, the fresh air, the snow, and the lore as well as the romance of skiing. Those would have to count as reinforcing consequences.

More Lessons

Our next lesson took place some two or three weeks later at a small ski area in Oregon known as Spout Springs. I didn't know it at the time, but it was the starting point for the skiing and teaching career of Joe Wagner who has had such a profound impact on the ski industry in Utah. He may have been at Spout Springs when I first took lessons there but I was such a novice I probably never encountered him. I didn't get to know him, and then not very well, until much later in Utah.

But, once again, I digress. The three of us took group lessons in different groups together for about six weeks. They were using the graduated length method, or GLM, at the time and so we started out on very short rented skis. It was embarrassing but effective because we didn't have so much ski to turn right off the bat. Quite clearly, the ski school was shaping our skiing behavior but neither we, nor they, thought so at the time. We were just having fun.

What I remember most about those lessons was down-, rather than up-, unweighting the skis. Of course, that movement was a bit advanced for me at that point, but they insisted so I gave it a try.

As experienced skiers and ski instructors know, to down-unweight the skis, you lighten them just before the turn with a down-, rather then up-, movement. Of course, you have to be up in order to move down, and I was almost always in a crouched position. I don't know which is easier but both are effective in lightening the skis. At that time, I had difficulty with either one so it really didn't matter. It was, perhaps, a bit too early in the shaping process.

By the end of the six weeks, we were all three making rather passable wedge christie turns, if not an open parallel turn from time to time, and were ready for another ski adventure, sort of a rite of passage. For that, we went to Anthony Lakes which was about a two and a half hour drive from our home in Walla Walla, Washington. Behavior established under one set of circumstances occurs under other, similar, circumstances. It generalizes as in going from Spout Springs to Anthony Lakes.

It was exciting to ski a new ski area, even though it was primarily on green and easy blue runs, and perhaps another one of the many reasons that people give for taking up skiing in the first place, the adventure. It, too, can be a reinforcing consequence when you try out new skills successfully or even unsuccessfully on new terrain. Sometimes they are reinforced and, sometimes, they aren't as with variable ratio schedules of reinforcement.

I remember ending the season having trouble with side-slipping and my daughters told me

"Dad, you look like a Christmas tree when you ski".

"What do you mean"?

"You're all bent over at the waist and so, with your ski parka on and ski poles in each hand, you look like a fir tree moving down the hill".

"Well, I guess I'll have to work on that".

I didn't know then, but do now, that skiers and especially ski instructors are always "working on their skiing". In addition, of course, my daughters were beginning to discriminate good from not so good skiing.

Intermediates

We continued to ski at Spout Springs for another three or four years with occasional trips to White Pass in Washington, Timberline at Mount Hood in Oregon, and Schweitzer as well as Brundage in Idaho; my parents owned a home on Payette Lakes and lived there year 'round. Anne and Jayne were becoming pretty good skiers but I, of course, still looked funny on my skis.

So, I took more lessons but not, as before, on a regular basis. In particular, I remember one lesson with Dorrie Graner who had taught for some time at Spout Springs and who later became the ski school director there. She tried to help me eliminate a stiff down hill leg at the end of the turn and was more or less successful. However, her success was not complete because I don't think I was ready to hear what she was telling me about it.

As experienced ski instructors know, "being ready to hear" what they are telling you makes a difference no matter how good the instruction might be. How that fits in to behavior theory isn't all that clear, but it may have to do with an already established repertoire of behavior. If it is incomplete to that point, further instruction may fall on deaf ears.

It may also have something to do with discrimination training. Seeing, hearing, tasting, touching, and smelling are things that we do. We do them with our senses. They occur along with other things that we do when we ski. They are covert, but they occur along with the overt behavior of skiing itself.

As a result, it wouldn't be too surprising that they are also affected by the consequences of what we do when we ski. Whatever reinforces it reinforces them.

In other words, seeing and hearing in particular (as well as proprioception) may be differentially reinforced along with the differential reinforcement that a ski instructor arranges for us during the lesson. Thus, when he or she says "Put more pressure on the outside ski at the start of the turn but absorb that pressure toward the end of it", we may not see it, and hear it, and feel it until some other behaviors are already well-established. On the other hand, there may be some already well-established behaviors that interfere with it.

Toward the end of that lesson with Dorrie, I asked her if I could be considered an intermediate skier and her reluctant agreement. Of course, anyone who has completed a beginning series of lessons is an intermediate skier, but I guess I needed to hear it from an official source as a reinforcing consequence. Nevertheless, I felt I was making progress despite my imperfections and that feeling may have been sufficient to keep me skiing and taking lessons.

On another occasion, I took a lesson with Tom Hale. He is a long time accomplished skier and ski instructor at Spout Springs and, later, at Ski Bluewood. I think he tried to get me to prepare sooner for the next turn because what I remember about that lesson was him skiing behind me yelling "Turn, turn, turn, turn" all the way down the ski run from the big chair at Spout Springs. I suppose he did that because I had developed the habit of "shopping" the next turn, that is, finishing one turn and then looking for the next one before getting ready to make it. Once again, I may not have been ready to hear what he was telling me because the habit of "shopping" the turn stayed with me for a long time. Some habits take longer to eliminate than others perhaps because of their reinforcement history or schedule of reinforcement.

Ski Bluewood

Eventually, the focus of our skiing turned to Ski Bluewood near Dayton, Washington. It is a small ski area about as close to our home as Spout Springs, but it had more challenging terrain and we considered ourselves ready for it.

Ski Bluewood is about fifty miles from Walla Walla and, like Spout Springs, is in the Blue Mountains. It has a top at about 5700 feet and a vertical drop of 1100 feet whereas Spout Springs has a top at about 5500 feet and a vertical drop of only 600 feet. Snow quality is about the same but the differences in height make for large differences in terrain. The shift in focus from one ski area to the other may simply illustrate how it happens that we go where the reinforcers take us.

More Lessons

Some time after our shift from Spout Springs to Ski Bluewood, I was in a lesson with either Brad Anderson or his wife, Kay

Mead, who helped to correct my stance on the skis. Brad and Kay directed the ski school at Ski Bluewood, were fully certified ski instructors, and very good skiers. I can remember them saying (where remembering is also something that we do and is explained by the same behavior principles),

"All right now, Jay, stand tall and well-balanced over your skis".

"Like this"?

"Taller".

"Okay"?

"Now, take a deep breath and exhale. As you exhale, relax your shoulders and sort of settle on the skis".

"Like this"?

"Yes. Now, bend at the knees instead of the waist and round your shoulders a bit like a boxer".

"Do you feel the difference"?

"Yes".

"Good. Now ski".

"Can't".

"Why not"?

"Too awkward".

"Well, keep working at it. That's where you need to be on your skis. Come back to that position and how it feels each time you ski or make a turn. Those feelings are important".

"Why"?

"They tell you whether you are correctly balanced on the skis".

Clearly, they were teaching me to discriminate both the internal and external cues for a balanced stance and were more or less successful at it. It took a while but, eventually, I was able to stand on the skis in a well-balanced position.

A Transition

At about this time, Anne and Jayne were entering high school or had already done so and were becoming pretty good skiers. As a result, when we skied they often went off together or with their friends rather than ski with me. I was either too slow, didn't ski well enough, or it was too embarrassing to be seen skiing with their father.

Once in a while, I would catch a glimpse of them from the chair lift and was astonished one year to notice that Jayne was no longer "in the back seat". She was well-balanced over the skis, dancing with the mountain. That is another of the reasons that people give for skiing and has to be a reinforcing consequence, to be able to dance with the mountain.

Anne, too, had become a very good skier and, in fact, had started to teach kids in the ski school at Ski Bluewood. Eventually, while in college, she became fully certified which lends further credence to the notion that we go where the reinforcers take us although it may require that you be young enough to do it.

Love Interest

Given those circumstances, it wasn't too surprising that my life took another direction. I met Barbara Jones. There had been others, but she has lasted the longest. In fact, some twenty years later, I had to admit to myself and to her that, like it or not, she had become the love of my life.

Actually, we met on the tennis court and, at one time, were ranked fourth or fifth in mixed doubles by the regional tennis association for the Pacific Northwest. However, that ranking, it must be noted, was based almost entirely on the number of sanctioned tournaments that we entered and not on how many we won. Nevertheless, we could claim a history of reinforcement for playing tennis together.

She also liked to ski along with a whole bunch of other things like dancing, running or jogging, bicycling, camping, hiking, rock climbing, and mountaineering. Indeed, it could be said that we had a lot in common except for rock climbing and mountaineering. There were simply some things that I didn't need to do. That is, there are limits to what we may find reinforcing.

Europe

Some few years of travail after we met, we were married and, a few years after that, were off to Europe. I had earned a sabbatical leave and could work on my project almost anywhere. So, we took the opportunity to see, and to ski, some of the world.

We went to (where else?) Austria. That choice was based in part on the history of skiing and the Arlberg technique, but only in part. It was also based on the lore and the romance of "skiing the Alps". Being able to do that and then to say that you have done it has to be a reinforcing consequence for any serious skier. Finally, it was also based on the fact that almost all of the ski areas were accessible by train. Ease of access makes skiing itself easier. Once again, we go where the reinforcers take us.

So, we "skied the Alps" all the way from Bad Gastein, to Schladming, to Kitzbuhl, to Haflekar, to Patcherkofl, to the Stubai Gletcher, to Axamer-Lizum, to St. Anton, Zurs, and Lech, to St. Christophe in Austria, to St. Moritz, Diavolezza, Corviglia, Pontresina, and Lagalb in Switzerland. There was also a brief excursion over the Brenner Pass to a small ski area in Italy called Sterzing or, if you are Austrian, Ratschings since the Austrians still consider it to be a part of Austria rather than Italy.

Along the way, we met through tennis and skiing Hugo Nindl who had skied the World Cup circuit for several years and Klaus Heiddiger who was a "technician" or slalom skier for the Austrian National Ski team. They were both residents of Axams, a little village about a half-hour out of Insbruck. We lived there in a pension about three miles below Axamer-Lizum, the site of the 1964 and 1976 Winter Olympic Games.

We left this country as intermediate skiers and returned as, perhaps, intermediate-advanced skiers and, while we gained a lot of skiing experience, it didn't seem to improve our skiing all that much, at least not mine. Nevertheless, we had many pleasant memories of skiing and the Austrian alps where remembering is another one of those things that we do. Of course, we were also able to talk about those memories. From that standpoint, our repertoire of skiing behaviors had increased immensely.

In somewhat different terms, we had achieved our goal of "skiing the Alps". To set a goal in the first place is, in the language of behavior analysis, to arrange a "contingency of reinforcement". A "contingency of reinforcement" consists of the antecedents to a behavior, the behavior itself, and the consequences of the behavior, the ABC's of behavior.

In this case, the antecedents to the behavior were setting the goal and all of the preparation that went in to planning the trip. The behavior itself was the travel as well as the skiing that we were able to do. The consequences were that we achieved that goal, returned to our home, and could then relate, in words and pictures, what we had achieved along with whatever changes occurred in our skiing behavior along the way.

To set a goal and achieve it is to be reinforced by that achievement as a consequence, and it then allows us to go on and do other things such as set other goals as a reinforcer. On the other hand, there is something to be said for the reinforcing effect of the journey itself when goals are not reached. There are lots of things that happen along the way to the goal that are reinforcing, such as seeing new sights and meeting new people, even though a major goal is not achieved. In this case, it was but, in life, not always.

Teaching Skiing

A year or two after returning from our trip, Barbara decided to start teaching skiing. There is no better way to learn a subject than to teach it and no one was more dedicated. She studied the manuals, watched the videos, took the clinics, prepared for exams, lived, breathed, skied, and taught lessons. Her daughter Meredith, who had accompanied us on our European trip, joined her from time to time at least to work with the kids in the ski school.

I, on the other hand, had some years earlier taken a course at the community college about teaching skiing from Walt Chauner who, in its early days, was the ski school director at Ski Bluewood and later moved to Beaver Creek in Colorado. He, of course, was one of the Bridger Bowl boys from Montana who, along with P J Jones had such an impact on the development of the United States demonstration team. Some already has been, but more will be, said about P J as we go along because he became one of Barbara's heroes although they are not related.

At the time I took the course from Walt, I was already committed to a very different teaching career and so didn't follow through to teach skiing. I did take one or two clinics from him later and remember, in particular, his liberal use of conditioned reinforcement.

Conditioned reinforcement was not mentioned earlier as one of the major principles of behavior that make up behavior theory but is a big part of it. A conditioned reinforcer is a word like "Good" that is reinforcing because it has been paired with other reinforcers or more primary reinforcement such as food. The word may start out somewhat neutral but then become reinforcing because of that pairing with other reinforcers. Walt was very liberal in his use of conditioned reinforcers, so much so that they sometimes didn't have the effect that he wanted them to have much like P J who was given a role of toilet paper with "Nice Turns!" printed on every square.

Nevertheless, his clinics could only be described as "electric" because they moved along so well and involved such lively exchanges between participants. There was a lot of skiing and just the right amount of talk.

But, once again, I digress. Barbara's ski teaching career took off, and I was left standing. Oh, we still skied together from time to time, but she became so immersed in the process of becoming certified that I sometimes seldom saw her on our trips to Bluewood except during local clinics for ski instructors. Then, I would tag along to ski with her and, of course, to receive some free instruction.

After a few years of that, Brad Anderson who usually led those clinics looked at me and said "There will be no more free lunch". I took that to mean "Either join us or don't come back". So, I joined them by taking the hiring clinic the next season.

By that time, I had been skiing for over twenty years and was a pretty good skier but perhaps only an advanced intermediate. I attributed that to the fact that I hadn't started skiing until I was in my early forties and, while in fair shape and a decent athlete, had muscles that weren't all that eager to learn. Teaching skiing added a whole new dimension to my skiing and helped me to get out of the intermediate rut.

Certification

By the time I started teaching skiing, Barbara was already certified at level two and was well in to the process for the next level. Because of the course I had taken with Walt and what little on snow instruction I had received connected with it, I didn't start the process of certification from scratch. Nevertheless, the hiring clinic introduced me to some new aspects of teaching skiing.

One was movement analysis. Behavior analysis is one thing. Movement analysis another. Discriminating what the feet are doing was not that easy for me, and still isn't, but I was able to see what they were doing at beginning levels. At least I found out enough that they took me on as a novice instructor.

Another aspect of teaching skiing was that it had to do primarily with motor skills. Prior to that, my teaching had been about intellectual skills and, while they are also important in skiing, are less so than helping people learn how to use their muscles. The role of shaping as a principle of behavior is much more pronounced when teaching the motor skills of skiing.

By the end of that season, I took and passed the examination for level two and was so in to the process of certification that I wrote an account of what I had accomplished for the professional ski instructors of the Northwest (PSIA-NW) newsletter. Clearly, Barbara was going where the reinforcers were taking her and dragging me, although not kicking and screaming, along with her.

On Becoming a Professional Ski Instructor of America

I am becoming a professional ski instructor of America. That fact, in itself, is not particularly remarkable. Lots of people are becoming ski instructors of America. What may be remarkable in my case is that I started when I was more than sixty years of age.

Why? Well, there are a number of reasons no one of which is necessarily true. One is that I have been skiing for more than twenty years and was ready for a change; teaching skiing is a way to experience it differently and, at the same time, improve your own skiing. Another is that my wife has been teaching skiing for a number of years and, as a result, we have not been skiing together as much as in the past; I thought we might be able to correct that if only by skiing together in clinics.

Still another reason for becoming a ski instructor is that I have developed a concern about health and fitness over the past several years and teaching skiing requires that you maintain at least a better than average level of fitness; consequently, it provides still another incentive to get, and stay, in shape. Finally, I have been impressed by the kind of people who teach skiing; most of them are bright, articulate and knowledgeable, and have accomplished other things in their lives. Another incidental consideration is that the technical director at our ski area was tired of my "free loading" when my wife invited me to come along on ski school clinics.

Since I have skied for more than twenty years and have taken a good many ski lessons during that time, I have learned quite a lot about it. As a result, during my first season of teaching, I felt that I should be at about a level two ski instructor not only with respect to my skiing but also with respect to technical knowledge. So, I asked the technical director at our area if that seemed like a reasonable goal. He replied "Well, you'll need to work at it but, with as much college teaching as you have done, teaching skiing should not be a problem. The problem may be in bringing that experience to bear on skiing". I agreed but still set that, with some misgivings, as my goal for the season.

I started where every aspiring ski instructor starts, with the hiring clinic at the beginning of the season. There were about thirty of us in the group, and we soon became acquainted through the common experience. Our training began with the video tapes published by the Professional Ski Instructors of America (PSIA) depicting beginning through level nine lessons.

In the process, we were introduced to the Center Line which I found to be extremely useful as the reference standard for the basic turns. In addition, many of us encountered for the first time the Basic Skills of balancing, rotary, edging, and pressure control movements and how they are related to the different phases of a turn as Skill Features; we might have been exposed to them in ski lessons but didn't necessarily know their names.

Since I was preparing to take three examinations that first season, from December through March I woke up each morning with a litany of questions and answers that I would ask myself about the Skill Features of a Wedge Turn, the Wedge Christy, the Open Parallel, and the Dynamic Parallel turns; visions of centerline (rather than sugar plums) danced in my head that Christmas. In addition, I would rehearse time and again the structure of the American Teaching System including the Skiing Model and the Teaching Model and how the system blends student behavior, instructor behavior, and lesson content into student outcomes.

My morning litany also included the Skier's Responsibility Code describing how skiers are to conduct themselves when they are skiing; in that sense, it is a set of ethical standards for skiers. These standards have been adopted to make skiing safer for those who participate. As such, they help to illustrate the extent to which ski instruction is guest oriented and service driven.

The Registered Level Examination was taken at the local ski area and consisted of five or six questions to be answered in writing. That is, it was a "take-home examination". Nevertheless, it required some thinking about, and application of, the Centerline as well as the Skill Features of Centerline turns. It also required that we know the signs for the ski runs and trails used at the local area which, because I didn't know them all off hand, I had to go out and find; it was a useful exercise because, in doing so, I looked at the terrain more closely and became better acquainted with it. In addition to the written examination, there was a requirement for having completed the hiring clinic as well as teaching a number of ski lessons.

The second, Level I, examination was also taken at the local ski area. However, it consisted of some more instruction in the form of watching and discussing the first PSIA video tape on ski lessons through level six, a written examination in the form of multiple choice items, and an on snow appraisal of "school figures", that is, the wedge turn and wedge christy and how well they conformed to the standards provided by the Centerline. There was also an assessment of "free skiing" in addition to the requirement of having taught more ski lessons.

Three of us took the examination, and our woman examiner (Kay Mead) was very thorough. It was her first time, and she made sure that we knew what we were talking about when we made reference to the Centerline and Basic Skills concepts. She also made sure that we could do the school figures and that our free skiing would not embarrass the ski school.

Additional preparation for the third, or Level II, examination involved attending the two day Pacific Northwest Divisional Academy, a one day Divisional Clinic at the local ski area, a two day Divisional Ski Racing Camp, and a two day Divisional Symposium. None of them was required for passing the Level II examination, but my wife was getting ready to take the examination for Level III and so both of us were in "exam mode". That is, we felt that it would be to our advantage to attend.

It was. In addition to meeting a good number of other ski instructors, Examiners, and Technical Team members, the two day Divisional Academy helped to refine our skiing, especially mine. I learned some patience in long- and short-radius turns. It was a revelation to discover that edging and pressuring the ski is a gradual process throughout the turn rather than something that happens all at once at the beginning of the turn.

The one day Divisional Clinic at our local ski area was conducted in fresh, heavy spring snow and the ski instructors in my group learned some new techniques for skiing it as well as receiving some additional instruction on our "school figures" especially wedge turns and wedge christies in those snow conditions. The clinic ended with a focus on our free skiing and, in particular, our open parallel turns. Our clinic leader did an impressive series of hop turns to illustrate how a hop can redistribute, and maintain, weight over the skis.

The Racing Camp was an indoctrination, at least for me, into the techniques, or mysteries, of skiing a giant slalom race course. In it, I discovered that many skiers, when skiing gates, keep their shoulders square to the skis throughout the turn instead of keeping their shoulders faced down the hill and letting their skis turn in and out under them. However, I didn't learn the lesson all that well because I "caught a tip" early in one of the runs and ended up with a bent ski. Nevertheless, I finished the run on that ski while it chattered around the remaining gates.

At the Divisional Symposium, my wife and I took an all day clinic on "skiing the bumps" at the conclusion of which we were both ready for a hot tub and a long nap. However, in another clinic the next day, we again were physically challenged and worked on refining elements of the ski turn with P J Jones who not only gave us some exercises for side slipping into the new turn but also impressed us with his teaching style; clearly, he has mastered the art of ski teaching and sets a high standard.

The weekend of our respective examinations dawned with spring clouds and snow storms. We each encountered three different examiners over the two day examination period; a take-home written examination had been submitted earlier with our application and fee. Each examiner assessed our technical knowledge of skiing, our teaching skills, and our school figures along with our free skiing; of course, my wife was in a different group since she was taking the examination at the next higher level.

Saturday was intense since we were graded by one of the examiners in the morning and another one in the afternoon. Sunday was not quite so anxious because there was only one examination period scheduled in the morning and then all we had to do was wait for the results to be announced at three o'clock that afternoon. We free skied while we waited and did what we could to not think about the outcome. Meanwhile, our ski school "support group" assembled to congratulate or commiserate depending upon the outcome.

Most of us had a sense of how well we had done but, of course, were more hopeful than certain until the results were handed to each one of us individually. When I received mine, I read it and sat staring at the summary sheet for a few minutes. I had passed but it took a while for that fact to register. I thought I was well prepared and that I would pass but it took some time to realize that I wouldn't need to wake up the next morning rehearsing all the things that I had learned in preparing for that moment; no more visions of Centerline, at least for a while.

It was over, as was the ski season, and I was a little let down. What was I going to do for an encore? I doubted very much that

I would ever qualify for, and take, the Level III examination, although it was certainly something to work at whether or not it ever came to pass. Nevertheless, I had learned a lot more about skiing and especially how to teach it that first season, and I looked forward to the next one with great anticipation.

Behavior Theory
and
Becoming a Ski Instructor

Of course, other interpretations are possible but this account clearly supports the proposition that ski instructors not only go where the reinforcers take them but that we also arrange conditions for reinforcers to occur. That is, we control and, in turn, are controlled. For example, we take a hiring clinic after being informed that there will be no more "free lunches", are hired, and then not only can we teach skiing but we can also take ski school clinics without such comments.

Similarly, we set a goal of becoming a level two instructor, or, we arrange a contingency of reinforcement for becoming one, and when we do are then able to teach higher levels of students. We prepare for examinations by taking clinics, or academy, or symposium, or racing camps and are then able, but not always, to ski better and to pass examinations. When we ourselves control the environment and it, in turn, controls us we have a case of self-control but more about that later.

A Note on Verbal Behavior

What you have encountered here so far has been verbal behavior. It has been my verbal behavior but also yours. If you continue reading, you will encounter more of it. Reading and writing are verbal behavior. They are about words.

Many years ago, B. F. Skinner wrote an entire book about *Verbal Behavior*. I will spare you the details. Suffice it to say that he treated verbal behavior like any other behavior. It is something that we do that is explained by the same laws and principles as any other behavior, or, it is shaped up and maintained by contingencies of reinforcement.

Reading, writing, talking, and thinking to the extent that we think in words are all verbal behavior. People talk. Sometimes, they listen. Listening, too, is verbal behavior. It has to do with words.

Sometimes people talk and have something to say. Sometimes people talk and don't have anything to say. Sometimes, when they talk and write about their exploits, they have something to say. Sometimes, they don't. When they are more inventive, they still may have something to say.

However, they may sometimes be so inventive that they are called liars or storytellers. That may happen when there is no correspondence between what they say and what they have done. The verbal behavior of liars and storytellers may be entertaining, but it is not informative. Nevertheless, it still may have been shaped up and maintained by contingencies of reinforcement. They are reinforced by our listening or reading, and we are reinforced for our listening by their telling of stories.

Then, of course, there are braggards. Like lying and storytelling, bragging is also something that people do. It, too, is verbal behavior. It, too, is about words.

Some years ago, a lineman for one of the Super Bowl teams was interviewed on television a short time before the game. In that interview, he talked about winning but not just about winning the game. He talked about winning "bragging rights" for the year following winning the game. Bragging rights are, of course, the right to brag about winning the game, something that football players do.

Bragging isn't altogether bad but to talk is one thing, to brag another. According to a dictionary definition, to brag is to talk boastfully, or, to boast. To boast, in turn, is to vaunt oneself or one's possessions; to brag. A second meaning for boast is to possess or display, especially with pride.

Now, there are of course people who talk about what they have done when they have, and even when they haven't, done it. As is said, talk is cheap. There are also those who brag about what they have done when they have and even when they haven't done it. And, there are those who boast about what they have done when they have and even when they haven't done it. Talking or writing, bragging, and boasting are closely connected.

Sometimes, we may try to talk and to write about what we have done to illustrate something else such as behavior theory. That is what I have tried to do here. In the process, I have sometimes felt some pride in those accomplishments but not always. Of course, pride is also something that we do and is explained in the same way as other behavior.

Sometimes I have simply felt that I was relating the facts. Nevertheless, I have frequently walked a fine line here between talking or writing, bragging, and boasting. Whether I have, in the process, succeeded or failed in relating the facts is up to the reader to judge. The more significant objective has been to illustrate the ways in which behavior theory helps to explain our day-by-day, or run-by-run, skiing behavior. If I have succeeded in that, I gladly risk bragging and boasting. In the great scheme of things, if there is one, it really doesn't make all that much difference. All of our feeble efforts may pale by comparison.

Canada

Skiing is not only reinforced by its consequences in the form of new sights and sounds but is also a reinforcing consequence. This fact is clearly illustrated by our skiing the next season in Canada.

We hadn't intended to but snow conditions in our part of the country were terrible. They had started out with great promise. Almost all of the ski areas were loaded early and often with great dumps of snow. However, it soon disappeared when what we locals refer to as the "Pineapple Express" came rushing through and melted it all away.

The "Pineapple Express" is like the "Fhon" in Austria. It is a warm wind that blows through the mountains and not only melts the snow but leaves the inhabitants feeling somewhat depressed. I am not sure whether their depression is from the loss of snow or something else but, in our case, it sent us searching.

Our local ski area, Ski Bluewood, lost nearly all of its snow in early January and the runoff was so great that it washed out at least one bridge that gave access to it. So, in order to ski, we had to look elsewhere.

Our first trip took us to Mount Hood Meadows in Oregon, but it lost its snow while we were on our way to ski it. A weather report said that a rain and ice storm was on its way in to the Columbia Gorge but that snow conditions at Mount Baker in Washington were excellent. So, we chased it through Portland, Oregon through Seattle, Washington to Mount Baker. That trip covered almost a thousand miles when you include the return to Walla Walla.

Not only was it a long distance, but we had superb skiing conditions for only one day. A storm hit Mount Baker the night following our one day of skiing, melted the snow, kept raining, and we returned home. All of that traveling and driving for one day of skiing gives a clear sense of the powerful reinforcing effect of skiing behavior. It is a consequence of travel and, in turn, increases the likelihood of traveling.

For example, while snow conditions where we lived were abominable, reports were good from Canada. So, a few weeks later, we took off for Alberta and British Columbia. Just before we crossed the border, Barbara was stopped by a traffic cop which shows that there are both punishing as well as reinforcing consequences for driving, or traveling, behavior.

We went from Walla Walla to Lake Louise to Sunshine Village to Panorama to Kimberly, and were able to fit in some helicopter skiing out of Panorama. However, the distance was well over a thousand miles round trip which says something more about skiing as a reinforcing consequence.

Several weeks later, we needed another skiing "fix" and so took a tour with Paul Jones and a group to Sun Peaks in British Columbia. He is a good host, we had a great time, and on the way back Barbara and I skied Apex, Big White, and Red Mountain before returning to Walla Walla. All told, we traveled a little over thirteen hundred miles on that trip.

However, we weren't finished. That year the symposium for the Pacific Northwest Division of PSIA was at Whistler-Blackcomb. So, once again, we were on our way back to Canada and British Columbia where Barbara found her way on to the cover for the divisional newsletter along with P J Jones and Jeff Cordell among others. Round trip mileage was about a thousand miles, but we were finished for the season. We had chased snow and were reinforced for doing it, but it hadn't been easy and involved no little expense.

A Note on the Problem of Purpose

Believe it or not, the foregoing account of our Canadian exploits raises a philosophical problem. I will spare you the details as I did earlier with verbal behavior.

Suffice it to say that our exploits could have been expressed in the language of purpose but deliberately were not. That is, we could have traveled those distances *in order to* ski or we could have traveled those distances *and were able* to ski. Obviously, the language used was the latter and it avoided the problem of purpose. It kept the analysis more parsimonious, or, simple.

Briefly, the problem of purpose has to do with whether it occurs in behavior or whether we impose it on behavior by way of language. Since there is no way to know whether purpose is there or whether we put it there, we can avoid the problem by using "and" rather than "in order to". In addition, of course, the latter is more in keeping with behavior theory and behavior analysis.

Utah

The next ski season, Barbara and I went to Utah. I had another sabbatical leave. When we went to Europe, I worked on a behavior theory of learning as a theory of knowledge. No one was interested. This time, I worked on common sense as a behavior. What I found out was that it is not all that common and that behavior analysts haven't done very much research on it even though they say they have tried to use it. Nevertheless, I needed a university library for that purpose, and the University of Utah was only a short distance from some six or eight ski areas. So, we went to Deer Valley and Park City.

We did so on the advice of Paul Jones and with his recommendations. He felt that there were more good skiers per unit of ski area in Colorado and Utah than anywhere else in the United States just as, so it has been said, there is more history per square meter in Austria than anywhere else in the world. Utah was more accessible.

Paul Jones, P J, is a remarkable character. For those of us who are a bit older, he is like a rock star with his own following. For those who aren't, he is an older gentleman whose skiing, though elegant, is a bit dated. Of course, as he says, they may not know that good skiing is good skiing regardless of the skier's age.

P J was born and raised in Montana and started his skiing as well as ski teaching career at Bridger Bowl. It was there he became acquainted with Walt Chauner who was mentioned earlier as one of my clinic leaders and classroom teachers, but theirs is another story.

P J tells the story about himself that he was fired for some infraction or another by the then director of the ski school at Bridger Bowl but that it was not to take effect until after he had taught his afternoon lessons, which he still had left to teach. If that sounds like a non sequitur, it is. When he showed up for work the next day, he was treated as though nothing had happened, but he had still been fired. Sometimes, a good firing sort of clears the air.

He went from Bridger Bowl to Colorado where he soon became director of the ski school at Aspen and produced, among other things, a video about skiing that Barbara found entrancing. She was directed to it by Tom Hale whom you may recall gave me one of my first ski lessons at Spout Springs and yelled "Turn, turn, turn, turn" at me all the way down a run.

Barbara considered P J to have the "best feet" in the ski business and watched that video over and over again not just because the skiing was so elegant but also to discover how he made it look so easy. Apparently, she was right. He does have good feet, if not the best, because he was a member of the PSIA Demonstration Team for some fourteen years and is still one of the premier examiners in the Northwest Division of PSIA. Those who pass an examination from him know that they deserve it.

He has also become a good friend largely because of the many private lessons we have taken with him but also because, whenever we get the chance, we attend his clinics. Those clinics have become remarkable for their use of modern technology in the form of video cameras, disks, and computers thanks to the efforts of his friend Georgia Hale otherwise known as "Cookie". Between them, she is always right, and he never makes a mistake.

But, once again, I digress. That summer we went to Utah and interviewed at both Deer Valley as well as Park City. On the basis of those interviews, Barbara felt that she was better suited to Deer Valley while I chose Park City. They each have notably different terrain and clientele. So, we "hired on" as they say in the West for the next ski season thanks to Sal Raio and Craig "Roper" Pearson the directors, respectively, of those two ski areas.

Ski Teaching at Park City

Ski teaching at a large ski resort like Park City is a bit different than ski teaching at a "mom and pop" ski area like Ski Bluewood. The difference has to do with numbers. Up to then, I had of course taught a few private and group lessons but not in great numbers. That changed at Park City.

It has a ski school of over two hundred full- and part-time ski instructors and, that first season, I worked full-time. That meant that, once I had learned something about the terrain and the resort thanks largely to the efforts of Dave Thurgood and John Allen, I taught a lot of lessons. Dave Thurgood deserves special mention because he, whether inadvertently or by design, became one of my ski teaching mentors. He is a long time instructor at the resort and is noted for his efforts to avoid teaching. He would much rather just ski. However, he is also an excellent instructor and supervisors keep him busy.

On the other hand, John Allen became my skiing mentor. He was originally from Orofino, Idaho and was fully certified in addition to being a likable guy. Consequently, he seemed quite capable of helping me to improve my own skiing.

The lessons were in groups with a sprinkling of private lessons only here and there. Private lessons go to those who have developed a clientele over the years, are more highly certified, or some combination of the two. Nevertheless, I was still able to get a few out of my group lessons and from my supervisors who included Tom Pettigrew, Rob Greene, John DeBord, Mike Thurgood, and Karin Cousins.

Since by that time I was on the new shaped skis, Rob Greene in particular turned some of the older skiers on those skis over to me. The chief problem for many of them was, after so many years on longer straighter skis, over-rotation. A second was a lack of patience in the fall line. They frequently tried to make the turn all at once rather than waiting and letting the skis do it for them. The result was a skidded, rather than carved, turn.

A third problem was stemming the turn rather than carving it. So far as I could tell, a stemmed turn was a lazy turn. It meant that we have not moved the "inside half" of the body in to the direction of the turn which requires a "crossover" or "crossunder" movement of the body and the skis. More will be said about that later.

Perhaps the most common problem for other intermediate and advanced skiers was what is known in the business as "whole body rotation" where the turn is initiated with the shoulders rather than the feet. Correcting it sometimes requires going back to a wedge turn which many of them found difficult to do while others were reluctant to do it. It seemed to be too basic for them.

A second common problem was "gorilla turns" or "cowboy turns" where the feet are a shade too far apart even though the skier is making open parallel turns. The image is of a gorilla, or a bowlegged cowboy, as they move down the hill.

Then, of course, there is a third common problem of an advanced skier having their feet, ankles, and knees locked together so that they twist and skid their turns rather than carve them. The image, in this case, is of a snake slithering, especially through moguls.

There were other problems, of course, but for the most part I taught beginners in groups. Beginning lessons are a challenge. They are a challenge because a beginning group presents such a mixed bag of age, ability, and fitness. Nevertheless, they are the backbone of the ski industry and need to be taught so well that people come back for more. Indeed, beginners need to be led or directed toward the next lesson while they are engaged in the first, and that became a part of my approach.

Common problems with beginners were "the wrong boot syndrome" where the skier has their boots on the wrong feet and the "wrong foot shuffle" where the skier needs to be reminded to move the "other right foot" rather than the one they are moving. In addition, there is "the crossover step" where the skier "steps over" one ski with the other and then must get things untangled. There is also "the cold sweat takeoff" where the skier is sweating so much from exertion, and perhaps fear, that almost all of the outer layer of clothing comes off.

Then, of course, there is "the death wedge" where the skier is able to get the skis in to a wedge but is locked at the knees and can't get them out of it, "the falling down hassle", and "the getting up thrash". A more picturesque image may be "the bull fighter's break dance" where the skier is all arms and elbows, ski poles and skis, flailing around while trying to maintain balance. Finally, there is "the bent at the waist balancing act" that I had so much difficulty overcoming in my own skiing. One of the most effective ways for correcting them was gentle kidding and laughter which are, or course, also things that we do and have their own reinforcing consequences.

That ski season was a blur and ended too soon, but it was also busy and exhausting. I was glad when it came to an end. Nevertheless, I had learned a lot about ski teaching and looked forward to doing it again wherever that happened to be.

A Note on Common Sense

While my ski teaching at Park City had come to an end, so had my research on common sense. On my days off from teaching skiing, I did research on the subject at the University of Utah library about a half hour drive from where we lived in Park City. For those who are interested, once again I will spare you the details, but suffice it to say that common sense can be treated as something that we do rather than something that we have. Not surprisingly, it too is a behavior that is probably shaped up and maintained by contingencies of reinforcement.

That behavior appears to be coming to conclusions that anyone else would reach under the same, or similar, circumstances. As such, it is explained not only by way of contingencies of reinforcement for the behavior, but it also generalizes to other, similar, situations.

Consequently, the principles of positive reinforcement, shaping, and generalization are largely responsible for it. However, not much empirical research has been done on common sense as a behavior and so it remains a catch-all expression for something that we have as well as something that we do.

The results of my inquiries into it were never published. It, too, along with a behavioral theory of knowledge are gathering dust in my file of unpublished manuscripts.

A Young Man's Game

The next season, Barbara and I were back at Ski Bluewood. I was committed to one more year of half-time teaching on phased retirement from my real job and so set as the goal for the year to become fully certified as a ski instructor.

By then, I was well in to my sixties but, what the heck, stranger things have happened to people who are over sixty years of age. Among them are just teaching skiing let alone doing it at Ski Bluewood or Park City Mountain Resort.

Becoming fully certified meant that I would need to ski "all conditions and all terrain" and to teach all levels of skiers from beginners to experts. It seemed like a formidable task, but I thought I was up to the challenge. I wouldn't know if I didn't try. So, I tried.

As a result, aside from my ski teaching assignments, I took a lot of local clinics with the technical director at Ski Bluewood, Jeannot Poirot, and a good many regional clinics with clinicians assigned by PSIA Northwest. In addition, I skied with such notables as Craig Noble and Brad Anderson at Ski Bluewood as well as Nick McDonald and P J Jones of PSIA-NW. I worked hard at it and gave it my best shot.

Among the tasks to master were long and medium radius turns, dynamic short radius turns, short swing turns, edge set turns, hockey stops, linked hockey stops, pivot slips, hop turns, leapers, edge-wedge hops, upper- and lower-body separation, anticipation, side-slipping, side-slipping in a corridor, "falling leaf", skating, left and right one-foot turns, medium radius turns in moguls with absorption, moguls, steeps, powder, crud, and ice. In other words, all of the things that an expert skier needs to be able to do when they ski.

Along the way, I took at least two pre-exam clinics where I learned what I still needed to do to pass the examination. In the first, with Mike Philips, I found out that I needed more work on movement analysis to correct skier problems with their skiing. I also needed more work on my own skiing and, in particular, the transition from short radius turns to short swing turns and back again.

In the second, I learned from Larry Murdock that I really wasn't up to edge-wedge hops, steeps, moguls, and linked hockey stops. So, although I had passed the written, I didn't take the skiing and teaching examinations and decided, along with Barbara, that full certification was a young man's game, or a younger man's game, at least for me. Aside from that, I had reached the point where ski teaching had lost its charm. It was no longer the powerful source of reinforcement that it once had been. I just wanted to ski as much, or as little, as I could.

The Present

And so, that is where I am now. I still like to ski and am obviously still interested in skiing, but I have lost the fervor where fervor has to do with energy and is also something that we do. It's not that important to me anymore. In the language of behavior analysis, it is still a source of reinforcement, and I am still interested in the development of a specialty for teaching seniors, but there is some doubt whether I will actually do it. What the future holds remains to be seen but I am sure there is reinforcement in it somewhere.

V

Ski Teaching

The Thesis

The last section explained instances of my skiing behavior by way of behavior theory. Clearly, Freud was only partly right. We don't do the things we do because of sex. We do the things we do, including sex, because of their reinforcing consequences such as orgasms, which are something else that we do.

There is also the behavior itself. Being able to do one thing reinforces having done something else. For example, being able to ski reinforces whatever we have done before being able to ski such as paying money for lift tickets before being able to ski. Buying lift tickets without being able to ski doesn't make much sense just as buying lift tickets and not skiing doesn't make much sense. "Making sense" of something is, of course, also something that we do.

Or, again, we take a lesson before being able to ski. We couldn't ski without taking the lesson no matter how bad the lesson although there are some notable exceptions. That is, there are some people who put on skis and, simply, ski.

Or, again, we travel longer distances before skiing. We couldn't ski without being some place to ski. Finally, we may travel around the world before skiing the Alps. We couldn't ski them without being there. So, skiing itself is a reinforcing consequence for other behaviors.

Similarly, we ski and feel the excitement of skiing. We ski and feel the wind in our face and the movement through space. We ski and encounter new terrain on beautiful snow covered mountains. We ski and see new sights especially fresh tracks in the snow. We ski mogul fields and emerge unscathed. We ski the deep and feel like we are floating on clouds. We ski the steep and feel the fear in our gut but great satisfaction when we look back up the hill and see what we have done including overcoming the fear.

We ski and travel from one place to another. We ski and feel the rush of endorphins. We ski and breathe the fresh air. We ski and dance with the mountain. We ski and feel the adventure of it. We ski and feel good. We do one thing and are then able to do something else. Those are the reinforcing consequences of skiing. That is how behavior theory accounts for our skiing behavior. What remains is to show how it accounts for our ski teaching behavior.

To state it more clearly, the basic thesis is that behavior theory, which consists of a number of behavior principles, can be used to explain not only our skiing behavior but also our ski teaching behavior. So far, we have seen what that theory consists of and have used it to account for some instances of my skiing behavior and that of my loved ones over the years. What remains is to show how the theory accounts for the teaching of skiing. I propose to do that based on an examination of the lessons for skiers levels one through nine as outlined in the 1989 Skiing Handbook of PSIA.

A Note on the History of Ski Teaching

It is remarkable to note how much modern ski teaching is based on the Arlberg Technique developed by Hannes Schneider and Mathias Zdarsky at St. Anton am Arlberg in Austria although Schneider gets almost all of the credit. Otto Lang, in his *A Bird of Passage* (1994, p. 56), points out that the technique was "based on the linkage of the snowplow to the snowplow turn, stem turn, stem christiania (sic), and finally the high-speed christiania, which required a minimum of stemming". Of course, today we frown on stemming because it suggests that we are not well-balanced on the skis but, back then, it was quite acceptable. Indeed, they may have had to stem in order to turn those long skis. Compare that technique to the four basic turns of modern ski teaching, namely, the wedge, the wedge christie, open parallel, and dynamic parallel turns.

Level I

The lesson plan in the handbook for this level of skier outlines a shaping process but without saying so in words. Shaping, or response differentiation, is of course one of the basic principles of behavior theory stated earlier and involves successive approximations, with reinforcement, to some final performance. The final performance, or goal, is linked wedge turns with and without a traverse that then makes it possible for the beginning skier to ride a lift.

At this level, there are ordinarily introductions to the instructor, one another, and the equipment. After that, the beginner usually encounters some form of reinforcement for putting the boots on the right feet if only the negative reinforcement of reducing the pain when they aren't. That, of course, is punishment for boots on the wrong feet.

Then, they may be encouraged when they walk around in their boots, or make a step around turn in them, or side step up and down the hill on their edges. Clearly, those behaviors are the first elements in a shaping process that results in skis on their feet.

Before that can happen, however, they may ordinarily be encouraged, or directed, to put on the downhill ski by clicking in to it and then walking around some more on that one ski not only in a straight line across the hill but also in a glide as on a scooter. The one almost inevitably leads to the other as a naturally occurring reinforcing consequence. Sometimes, the "downhill ski" may need to be identified just as the "outside ski" or the "inside ski" in a turn may require identification with a higher level of skier.

Then, stepping that one ski to turn around or to move up the hill approximates doing it later with both skis and is another behavior likely to be encouraged not only by the instructor but by the effects it has in letting the skier see what is behind them. Those approximations are a key ingredient in the shaping process and they occur successively in different ways at all levels of ski teaching. A beginning lesson may simply be where it is most obvious.

Once they have clicked out of that ski and in to the other one, the stepping sequence may be repeated until they are ready for skis on both feet at the same time. Skis on both feet is a significant change and may result in a fear response.

If it does, the principle of respondent extinction may come in to play. Recall that fear is a respondent with both overt and covert features. Overt features include sweating, blanching, wide eyes, shaking, and falling down. Covert features are private but may include increased heart beat, butterflies in the stomach, anxiety, and difficulty breathing. They are evoked, or elicited, by at least some elements of the environment and those are paired with others. As a result, there may be a good number of them that evoke and sustain the fear behavior.

One way to implement the principle of respondent extinction is simply to have the skier stand with their skis across the fall line and then to click in and out of each ski several times, first one and then the other, starting with the uphill ski. Sidestepping up the hill may also help. That, in itself, may be sufficient to reduce the fear response but, if it doesn't, the instructor may need to devise some other more clever procedure until that happens. Fear reduction in the student is the reinforcing consequence for the instructor.

Once their fear has been brought under reasonable control, the next step in the shaping process is to get them to glide across the hill to a stop. That may take some doing but the reinforcing consequence for the student is the glide and the stop. They are able to do it. The reinforcing consequence for the instructor is also the glide and the stop. Their student is able to do it. Sidestepping up and down the hill may be a part of that sequence.

Then, of course, the student must "step around" for the next glide but, to do that, at some point they must face downhill. Facing downhill for the first time may also evoke a fear response and, once again, the principle of respondent extinction may need to be implemented.

This time, having them step into a wedge each time they make a movement downhill in the other direction on very shallow terrain may help to reduce the fear, if there is any, and perhaps eliminate it entirely. If it doesn't, once again the instructor may have to devise some other clever procedure that uses the principle.

At this point, the student or group may simply need some mileage otherwise referred to as practice. However, it needs to be supervised, and reinforced, practice or other behaviors may get established that have to be corrected later. The behavior to be established is the glide across the hill to a stop, perhaps a side step or two up or down the hill, the step around or "bull fighter" turn, and the glide to a stop in the other direction.

The result of the practice or mileage may be some spontaneous stepping turns in the other direction. When that happens, at least some of the students are ready for a wedge turn with and without stepping. To do that, they simply may need more reinforced practice under the guidance of the instructor. Regardless, they are well on their way to wedge turns and to linked wedge turns.

Level II

When that happens, they are at level two. Ordinarily, a beginning skier progresses from level one to level three in the first lesson. When they don't, their second lesson may be at level two.

At level two, the final performance, or goal, in the shaping process is linked and rounded wedge turns to a stop on shallow terrain. So, the skier continues to work on improving control with the size of the wedge and steering the skis in the direction of the turn they are making. They may also get to the point where they are ready to ride a beginner lift and to ski some of the easier green runs.

Before they get to that point, however, there may have been something that has held them back from progressing at the same rate as others in their original group that may need to be addressed. Some of those problems may have to do with the size of the steps in the shaping process that was used previously, how they learn, their natural or unnatural athletic ability, fear, fitness, or handicaps. Whatever it is, it has interfered with new learning and so needs to be dealt with.

In fact, if they are in a group lesson it may be necessary to return their ticket and encourage them to exchange it for a private lesson where they will receive more individualized attention. An alternative may be to have them work by themselves for a while, go on with the rest of the group, and then get back to them a short time later. Each ski area may have a different procedure for dealing with those who are not able to move along with their original group.

If they can, they are soon ready to ride a beginner lift. One way to introduce them to that is simply to have them stand and watch how others are doing it. The principle of imitation works very well here just as it has for all of the other behaviors that have been demonstrated previously and that they have been asked to do.

Indeed, imitation may be one of the principles that contributes most to the improvement of skiing behavior, aside from reinforcement, because it continues to affect it even when skiers are not in a lesson. Of course, it can also contribute to some very bad habits and, in particular, locking the feet together and slithering down the hill. Some younger skiers think that looks "really cool" and try to do it even though it may not be what their instructor is trying to get them to do. Clearly, even beginning and younger skiers go where the reinforcers take them.

One direction is up the hill on a chair lift where new terrain awaits their efforts. After they have watched others load the lift, a description of the steps in the procedure may further reduce any questions or anxiety or fear they may have about how it is done. In addition, having the lift operator slow it down or having them aid in the process may also facilitate getting the novice skier on the lift.

Once they are on the lift, there isn't much left for them to do except to see the new sights and then to get off at the top. Getting off at the top may pose its own problems because they may not be all that sure about the sequence of events that occurs before they are free of the lift.

Consequently, it is here that they may take their first fall if it hasn't happened before. If they fall, their first obligation is to get out of the way of those unloading behind them. That assignment may take many forms. One is crawling on hands and knees to the side of the unloading area. Another is scooting on their buttocks. A third is a one legged shuffle if they have lost a ski. Whatever it takes to get out of the way is in order at that point.

Once out of the way, perhaps the easiest method for getting them upright again is to have them remove the uphill ski and then simply stand up. After that, it is relatively easy to click in to the absent ski.

On the other hand, there are many who can get upright with skis on both feet with, and without, the use of poles. Usually, if no big fuss is made about falling down, the task of getting back up is not an issue. If it is, then the ski off one or both feet may be all it takes.

The lesson then continues with shaping linked and rounded wedge turns to a stop on new terrain. One of the simplest ways to accomplish that is for the instructor to lead the way by demonstrating how to do it and by letting the principles of shaping, positive reinforcement, and imitation have their way.

A Note on the Demonstration of Skiing Behavior

Whenever a ski instructor demonstrates a skiing behavior, he or she models it. That is, they rely on the principle of imitation. Eventually, imitation may be shown to be a form of conditioning in which a follower does what a model is doing because the follower's behavior is reinforced, not for following, but by the natural consequences of doing what the model is doing. In other words, the behavior of the follower is affected by the same reinforcers that affect the behavior of the model. As such, it may be called imitative conditioning rather than just imitation. Whatever the case, it still has a profound effect on behavior and especially skiing behavior.

For example, by leading the way in lesson two, the instructor not only shows how to perform some skiing behavior, he or she also shows how to control speed with the shape of the turn. Austrian ski instructors with their long ques of students may be teaching not only how to shape the turn as well as speed control but the rhythm and flow of skiing when they have their students follow them down a hill.

Beginning skiers may concentrate so much on the shape of the turn that they miss how it helps to control speed, and it may take a while before they are able to discriminate the two. Discrimination training, of course, involves differential reinforcement for one kind of behavior and extinction of another and so the particular skiing behavior may need to be identified and singled out by the instructor before it is reinforced. Then, he or she may have to do the same for speed control. While they normally occur together, they may also need to be identified and reinforced separately for the skier to see and feel the difference. Seeing and feeling are, of course, also things that they do as well as rhythm and flow.

Imitative Conditioning
and
Superstitious Conditioning

While imitative conditioning may have imitation as its outcome, the same may be true for superstition. To explain, it was proposed above that imitative conditioning may simply be a form of conditioning in which the follower is reinforced, not for following, but by the same reinforcers that affect the behavior of the model.

Superstition, on the other hand, may appear to be a failure of discrimination training in which training fails to establish a differential response between correlation and contingency. That is, we refer to a correlation between a response and reinforcement as superstition whereas a contingency between a response and reinforcement is operant conditioning.

Eventually, it may be shown that superstition is also a form of conditioning in which behavior is affected by the correlation between it and reinforcement rather than the contingency between it and reinforcement. That is, it is not a failure of discrimination training but a form of conditioning in its own right. As such, it may be called superstitious conditioning rather than just superstition. Whatever the case, it still has a profound effect on behavior and especially skiing behavior.

Level III

At level three, the final performance or goal of the shaping process is linked and rounded wedge turns with perhaps some matching of the skis toward the end of the turn. The skis are matched, of course, when they are brought parallel to each other.

Ordinarily, that process continues on newer and perhaps somewhat steeper terrain. As a result, it may be necessary to return to somewhat earlier steps in the shaping procedure.

One way to do that is with a fan progression. Fan progressions may be effective at all levels of ski teaching but especially at the level of wedge turns where a "fan" is the pattern that the progression leaves in the snow when the skier looks downhill at it.

A fan progression for the wedge turn may begin with the skier simply skiing in a traverse across the hill and playing with wider and narrower wedges to a stop. Then, they may step around to do it in the other direction.

After that, they may start the traverse in a wedge but point the skis slightly downhill. When they do that, they may feel a slight acceleration but then slow their speed by turning the skis back up the hill. The result is a very shallow wedge turn that uses the fall line but doesn't cross it.

If they do that across the hill, their track leaves a "garland" across the throat of the hill where a garland ordinarily refers to the wreath draped across the neck of the winner at the Kentucky Derby. Regardless, the track is a series of scallops across the hill in both directions if done properly.

The next step in the shaping process is to point the skis further down the hill but then steer them back up the hill to control speed. Speed control is, of course, the reinforcing consequence. At this point, the skier is once again in the fall line but has not crossed it. That progression continues until the skier has skied a "fan" of turns to the left as well as to the right.

By this time, they may have reached the point where, at the end of the garland across the hill, they are able to turn, or step, their skis in the other direction without coming to a stop. If they have, they are well on their way to linking the turns together one after the other to the bottom of the run.

If they haven't, they may need further work with the fan progression until all members of the group are able to link the turns in both directions. When they are able to do that, the lesson can then continue with linking and shaping the turn for speed control.

As the group becomes more and more adept at controlling the speed of the turn, some in the group may perform some spontaneous wedge christies as well as some open parallel turns. Those are to be encouraged, or reinforced, as well as being encouraging, or reinforcing, to the skier because those are what they are working for in the early stages of skiing.

If they don't occur spontaneously, the skier may need to be encouraged to simply make a wedge turn but then to match the skis after the fall line before starting the next one. With more mileage, they may all be making wedge turns with matching of the skis before starting the next turn by the end of the lesson.

The Ethics of Skiing
or
The Skier's Responsibility Code

By this time, they may have experienced a few close encounters with other skiers and so may be ready to hear about how to conduct themselves on a ski hill. That, of course, takes the form of the skier's responsibility code, or, the ethics of skiing.

In the language of behavior analysis, that code has to do with rule-following behavior where the rules function as cues to one kind of behavior rather than another. They are a form of discrimination training where, in the presence of one kind of cue, a behavior is reinforced and, in the presence of others, it is not reinforced.

Thus, for example, the rule to ski in control directs, or cues, the skier to control the speed at which they are skiing so that they can come to a stop whenever they may need to do so; the cue is speed. Similarly, the rule to stop at the side of a run directs him or her to get out of the way of other skiers when they come to a stop so that they do not obstruct the flow of traffic; the cue is the side of the run. The same may apply to the third rule to look up the hill before resuming skiing after they have come to a stop; the cue is other skiers.

On the other hand, the rule that the skier in front has the right of way makes that skier a cue to the one behind about where to make their next turn; the cue is the other skier. Similarly, the rule to observe all signs directs them to stay in bounds, or observe that trails merge, or to watch out for hidden obstacles the consequences for which may be punishment if they are ignored; the cue is the sign.

Finally, the last two rules have to do with equipment. One is about wearing a restraining device of some sort to prevent their skis, if they detach, from injuring someone else; the cue is the restraining device. The other is to find out how to load all lifts if they don't know how to do it; the cue is the lift.

Some of those rules are simply a matter of common sense if we knew what it was. Others are a matter of common experience. All may help to make skiing more enjoyable and satisfying, not to mention safer, for those who do it.

Level IV

At level four, the shaping process continues refining the wedge christie turn so that matching occurs earlier and earlier as in the shaping procedure. Initially, matching occurs more toward the end of the turn, then at about the fall line, and then just before the fall line with each turn starting from the wedge. Clearly, that is an instance of successive approximations to the final performance of wedging but then matching the skis before the fall line, or, a wedge christie turn.

Once again, a fan progression may help to facilitate the shaping process with the matching taking place first from a shallow wedge turn both left and right and then from steeper and steeper wedge turns until the turn is made almost straight out of the fall line. Newer and somewhat steeper terrain may help in this process because especially steeper terrain may increase speed and, when the skier turns to control speed, there may be some skidding. Skidding as well as matching are major features of the wedge christie turn.

So, somewhat steeper terrain is in order at this point because the skier is ready for it as well as sideslipping since skidding is a matter of slipping to the side. A progression for sideslipping is for the student to stand with both skis across the fall line on the uphill edges of both skis. While just standing still, they may then be encouraged to simply edge and release the edges of the skis at the side of the trail. The result, of course, is some slipping to the side from the standing position.

After some reinforced practice on both the left and the right side, they may then be encouraged to traverse across the hill on their uphill edges both left and right. The result should be two sharply edged tracks in the snow on the uphill side.

A third phase in the progression is for the student to once again stand at the side of a run on the uphill edges of the skis and then traverse across the fall line by edging and then releasing the edges of the skis alternately so that they feel what it is like to slip to the side while moving forward on the skis. At the end of the traverse, they may then look back to see what the track of their skis looks like when they edge and then release the edges of the skis. The result should be edged and smeared tracks in the snow in a garland across the hill.

As the shaping process continues, more and more of the traverse can be skidded and less and less edged until there is almost no edging. When that happens, they are sideslipping almost entirely.

After that, they may then go back to linking rounded wedge turns with matching and at sufficient speed to feel some skidding toward the end of the turn or as they are matching the skis before or after the fall line.

Once they have reached that point with some measure of speed but where it is under control, they may be ready and eager to try the turn with some skidding on new and steeper terrain including all green and some easier blue runs. At that point, they are ready to ski the mountain on most blue and almost all green runs. The shaping process of reinforcing successive approximations to the wedge christie turn is complete. They are ready for the next level of skiing.

Level V

At level five, the skier is able to ski the mountain on all green and most blue runs. However, they may do so with only an indifferent use of the pole touch. The wedge christie turn with pole touch is the final performance in the shaping process for skiers at level five.

A progression for pole touch at level five is for the skier to stand with both skis across the fall line at the edge of a ski run and then to just alternately touch the poles to the snow from a standing position. Then, they may be encouraged to do the same as they make a traverse across the run looking up from time to time to see that they are out of the way of other skiers. Reinforced practice, on both the left and right sides of the skier, is useful at this point and may consist of nothing more than their being able to do it.

Then, they may do the touching exercise on both the left and right sides to the count of three, one two three, one two three, for rhythm. Rhythm is another reinforcing consequence in skiing as in dancing. The next step may be to rise up a little on the count of two and to touch the pole lightly to the snow on the count of three.

After that, the next step in the progression is to count one, rise up on two, touch the pole and then turn on three. The count one, two, three, one, two, three is very much like the count of a waltz step and so may get incorporated into their skiing along with the pole touch and turn.

From that point, it is a fairly easy step to the touch and turn, touch and turn of level five skiing. More reinforced practice on all green and most blue runs will then prepare them for level six.

Level VI

Of course, some spontaneous open parallel turns may occur at almost any time in the shaping process and are to be identified and reinforced. However, they are the goal, or final performance, at level six where an open parallel turn occurs in a fairly wide stance with the upper body somewhat open to the downward slope of the hill. In other words, open parallel turns with pole touch are the objective at this level.

In many cases, that objective can be accomplished with an increase in speed as the instructor leads the way down the hill. When it can't be accomplished in that way, it may be necessary for the instructor to review what the skier has been able to accomplish to that point and then to state the goal and to demonstrate it.

Those who are not able to match the skis throughout the turn may still wedge, or stem, the turn at the beginning. If they do, they may be out of balance over the skis or "in the back seat". There is no easy, or sure, way to correct that problem except balancing exercises to get them to feel what it is like to be in balance on the skis.

One way to do that is, not surprisingly, another fan progression. This time, they may be asked to stand at the side of a run with both skis, once again, across the fall line. Then, while still standing, they may be encouraged to simply lift one ski and then the other alternately starting with the uphill ski. To accomplish that, they have to be in balance on the edged ski that remains on the snow.

Once they are able to do that on both the left and right sides, they may then be asked to step from the left to the right ski in a traverse across the hill both on the left and on the right sides. Extensive reinforced practice may be required before they can accomplish that efficiently although some may still be able to do it while "sitting back". It is easier if they are in balance.

Once they are well practiced at stepping, they may be asked to make the turn by stepping to the outside ski and then making the turn on that ski. Once again, that can still be done from the "back seat" but it is easier, or more efficient, if they are in balance.

As a rule of thumb, students who can lift the inside ski at any time during the turn are in balance, those who are forced to lift it especially at the start of the turn are not. It is a measure of fore and aft, as well as lateral, balance on the skis.

That progression may still not correct the problem. If it doesn't, more reinforced practice or mileage with a ski instructor may be required. An alternative is to talk about balance and to note that it can be fore and aft as well as side to side with a demonstration. The ideal, of course, is "lagonal", or lateral and diagonal, into the new turn and work on turns with pole touch in that direction.

However, any number of things may contribute to the problem including lack of preparation for the next turn as when Tom Hale shouted "Turn, turn, turn, turn" as we skied down a run. Consequently, there may not be any single method for correcting balance. Any one of them, or a combination, may correct it including whether or not the skier is ready to "hear" what they are being told when it happens as when I skied with a stiff downhill leg until I was able to hear Dorrie tell me to soften it at the end of the turn.

A Cautionary Note

By now, it may be abundantly clear that we are not exploring each and every way in which behavior theory may be applied in ski teaching. Rather, we are simply examining some of what might be considered the usual ways where it might apply. The purpose is not to write a teaching manual since that has already been done by PSIA and others. Nevertheless, it should not be too difficult to see from the examples that have been used here how the theory might apply to the nuances of ski teaching that have not been presented here. Behavior generalizes and ski teaching is no different than any other behavior.

Level VII

At skier level seven, we are rapidly approaching the limits of my ski teaching experience as well as my level of certification. However, in what preparation I have done to become fully certified, I have had some teaching experience with the upper three levels of skiers and so can continue to examine how behavior theory applies in ski teaching despite those limitations.

At level seven, the final performance of the shaping process is "short radius parallel turns in the fall line" as well as "medium and long radius carved parallel turns across the fall line". In addition, those turns are to be "applied to a wide variety of trails and conditions, including all groomed single black diamond runs".

Perhaps the most effective way to teach those turns at this level is with the principle of imitative conditioning. That is, after introductions and some discussion of what both the skier and the instructor want to accomplish in the lesson, the instructor may just say, "Follow my tracks", and ski off with a series of turns. That series might consist of those long, then medium, then shorter radius turns until the skier who is following makes a series of short radius turns with rhythm. Clearly, that progression is a shaping process because, if the student is able to do them, he or she is reinforced at the completion of each turn by completing the turn and doing the next one. In addition, of course, rhythm itself is a reinforcing consequence.

If the student is not able to do them, the instructor as well as the student may have detected where the student is having problems and work to eliminate them. One problem is stemming which, of course, is a balancing issue examined earlier.

Another problem may be preparation for the next turn which needs to occur more and more quickly as the radius of the turn decreases. Here, the reader may recall my experience with Tom Hale shouting "Turn, turn, turn, turn" as we skied down a run at Spout Springs.

Still another problem may be absorption. Short radius parallel turns can frequently generate forces that the skier has not encountered before. To control them, they may need to learn how to absorb them where to absorb is to swallow up; to cause to disappear or lose identity; to suck up as does a sponge; to take in; to engross or engage wholly; to receive without a recoil or other effect.

Absorption, like preparation, is something that we do and so can be taught with principles of behavior. One way to do it is with a progression which, of course, involves shaping or response differentiation.

For example, the skier may be asked to stand at the side of a run and then to simply sink down on the skis several times to illustrate the feeling of absorption when they do it. Then, they may be asked to let the skis come up to their chest as they ski over a bump just as Dorrie asked me to soften the down hill leg at the end of a turn. However, to absorb a bump, they need to let both skis come up as they go over it and to keep their upper body at the same level.

Next, they may be asked to do more than one bump in the snow like a car going over ruts in the road while keeping the upper body still. Then, they may be asked to ski a turn and to absorb the forces of the turn by letting both legs soften as they complete the turn. After that, they may be asked to ski a series of short radius turns with absorption of each turn as they ski it. The last phase of the progression may simply be a matter of reinforced practice with the instructor leading, and sometimes following, the turns of his or her client.

Level VIII

At skier level eight, the skier is at the advanced expert phase where the final performance of the shaping process is dynamic parallel turns. In addition, there is the matter of "adapting skills to the size of the turn and tactics in powder, variable conditions, and bigger bumps". Those are the teaching objectives, or goals, at this level.

Now, the difference between an open parallel turn and a dynamic parallel turn may simply be that the skier is more active on the skis. They are more dynamic. To be more dynamic may simply mean, in turn, that they are more proactive, rather than reactive, on the skis.

That is, they may be better prepared for the next turn rather than continuing to respond to the last one. As such, early preparation, or anticipation, may be the essence of the lesson at this level just as absorption might be thought of as the essence of the lesson at level seven.

To be prepared early for the next turn, may simply be a matter of anticipation where to anticipate the next turn is to take up, use, or introduce ahead of time; to deal with before another; preclude or prevent by proper action; to be before another in doing or acting; forestall; to foresee and do beforehand; to experience beforehand; to expect. As such, the downhill racer imaging the course before his or her next run may be the ultimate form of early preparation or anticipation.

Like absorption, anticipation is something that we do and so it can be taught with behavior principles. One way to go about it is to ask the skier to stand at the top of a run and to describe the next turn they are going to make, where they are going to start it, and where they are going to finish it by pointing out those phases of the turn in the snow. Then, they might be asked to ski it and to compare how it felt to their beforehand description. Accuracy is less important than the act of anticipating. Anticipation is the behavior being established and not description.

Next, they might be asked to do it for the next two turns, then four, and then an entire run while also talking about early preparation as well as anticipation. That is what the lesson is about, early preparation for, and anticipation of, the next turn and those for the remainder of the run. They may then be able to take that in to powder, variable conditions, and bigger bumps by way of generalization. If not, it may need to be taught under each of those conditions for what remaining time there is in the lesson.

Level IX

At skier level nine, the objective of the lesson is "all conditions, all terrain". More formally, the handbook describes it as "selecting tactics to enhance skiing in all snow conditions and terrain".

By this time, the skier has mastered the basic skills of edging, pressuring, and rotating the skis while remaining in lateral as well as fore- and aft-balance. They are also able to ski all groomed and un-groomed runs up to and including most double black diamonds or, as is said, the "steep and the deep". What remains, if they are even in a lesson, is to refine all of their turns under those conditions. Consequently, the lesson as always needs to be tailored to what they want out of it including new developments in ski technique and in ski teaching.

One sub-goal may be to refine long, medium, and short radius dynamic parallel turns especially carving. Another may be quickness, control, and speed changes in short radius turns.

Still another may be selecting the line they may want to ski in moguls which brings in to play the higher order skills of absorption and anticipation or preparation. Finally, they may simply want to ski with an instructor not only to see how their skiing compares but also to learn more about skiing that particular mountain. They have reached the point where they are free to do that or, to paraphrase an old well-worn expression, "they know the truth (or as much as we can know of it) and it has set them free".

Some Other Higher Order Skills

In addition to what has been referred to above as the "higher order skills" of absorption, and anticipation or early preparation, there are a number of others that might be given the same treatment at skier levels eight and nine. They are: rebound, rhythm, and flow in addition to crossover, crossunder, extension, and retraction.

Rebound refers to the use of some, if not all, of the energy from the last turn to unweight the skis for the next. From that standpoint, it is the opposite of absorption. There are times when absorption is appropriate, and there are times when rebound is appropriate and, sometimes, both.

For example, if the skier stiffens the knees in the fall line of the last turn, he or she will impact the snow during the completion of the turn with more force than if he or she softens them in the fall line. That counterforce is rebound, and it can be used to bounce and unweight the skis for the next turn.

Rhythm is a separate skill because it has to do with the tempo at which skiers make their turns. Some skiers may make a series of some four or five short radius turns followed by a series of some four or five medium radius turns while others may simply make a series of medium or longer radius turns all the way down the hill. The result is rhythm, or changes in it, and many skiers feel it when they say that skiing is like dancing with the mountain or, perhaps, dancing on it.

Flow has to do with continuity. To flow down the hill is to never be static on the skis, to never finish a turn and then to prepare for the next one but to always be preparing for the next or finishing the last. In other words, the skier is always busy on the skis if not in preparation for the next turn then in completion of the last one. There are no places in the turn where the skier is not doing something; there is a constant flow of movement down the hill.

Crossover refers to the skier deliberately moving over the skis in a lateral and diagonal direction into the next turn. It is the movement most commonly taught to beginning and intermediate skiers. Crossunder refers to the skier allowing the skis to come under his or her body in a lateral and diagonal direction into the next turn. The difference is a subtle one but advanced skiers can discriminate that difference and so the behavioral principle of discrimination training is at work when the ski instructor is teaching those skills.

To illustrate the difference, consider leaning the inside half of the body, the strong inside half, in a lateral and diagonal direction into the new turn as opposed to letting the skis drift under the body in a lateral and diagonal direction into the new turn. That is the difference between crossover and crossunder, respectively.

On the other hand, extension refers to lengthening the body while skiing by simply standing taller or by pushing the skis out and away from the body. The result is that the skier is more likely to maintain balance which may be the naturally occurring reinforcing consequence.

Similarly, flexion, contraction, or retraction refers to shortening the body while skiing by simply bending the knees and ankles more or by pulling the skis back and under the body. Once again, the result is that the skier is able to maintain balance as the reinforcing consequence especially at higher speeds and, perhaps, in the bumps.

If so, then another reinforcing consequence for either behavior may be that they help the skier to execute turns more accurately, more easily, or more quickly. Of course, extension and retraction may also combine with rebound and absorption with similar consequences.

To teach those skills may require nothing more than imitative conditioning especially since they are not likely to be taught until skiers have reached advanced levels of skiing. Thus, the ski instructor may simply describe each skill, demonstrate them separately, ask the skier to perform those behaviors, and then reinforce them when they occur correctly.

On the other hand, the instructor may rely primarily on imitative conditioning. That is, he or she may simply have the level eight or level nine skier follow his or her tracks down the hill. However, the principle of positive reinforcement may also be implemented when they observe that the student is employing those skills, or at least trying, and comment to that effect.

In addition, of course, the natural reinforcers of the turn may also help to shape those skills as when the turn becomes easier to make by using rebound, or the skier feels the rhythm of the turn by way of proprioceptive receptors in the muscles and joints, or their skiing becomes less herky-jerky.

Discrimination training as a principle of behavior may also come in to play at that point to help the skier discriminate those differences in their skiing which may not have been possible earlier. They may not have been ready for them.

VI

Conclusion

It may not have escaped the notice of those who have read this far that what has been presented here explains not only skiing and ski teaching behavior but living in general. Living is also something that we do. Life is about living. It is not about the bike, and it is not about the skis.

We are born, and the first thing that we do is bawl which has the reinforcing consequence of clearing our lungs. That, in turn, allows us to breathe. Bawling and breathing are things that we do. They are behaviors. Behaving is the mark of a living organism.

I will spare the reader from further details about what follows after bawling and breathing. Suffice it to say that one behavior with reinforcing, or punishing, consequences follows another with reinforcing, or punishing, consequences until we die. Living, or life, has a beginning, a middle, and an end.

Indeed, living is very much like the metaphor of the jigsaw puzzle. After the preliminaries of turning over the pieces, puzzling begins when we put the first two pieces together. It doesn't matter what those pieces are, that is the beginning. Putting those first two pieces together is something that we do. It has the reinforcing consequence of allowing us to see them together which, in turn, allows us to look for another.

Looking for another piece allows us to find it. Finding it reinforces looking for it which, in turn, allows us to put it with the first two pieces. Putting it together with the first two pieces is a behavior that follows looking behavior and so on to the last piece when we then may go on to make dinner or wash the dishes.

Variations can occur. For example, while looking for the third piece, we may find two others that fit together. Finding is a behavior that is reinforced by fitting the two new pieces together followed by a third and a forth that complete one part of the puzzle.

That part of the puzzle may then fit together with the first two pieces which, of course, is a reinforcing consequence that allows us to look for other pieces reinforced by the consequence of finding them reinforced by the consequence of putting them together. Once again, I will spare the reader from further details.

Suffice it to say that what has been presented here can explain skiing as well as ski teaching behavior but also puzzling as well as living behavior in general, or, life itself. No more could be asked of any theory.

The Problem of Circularity

At least one problem remains. It is the problem of circularity. The problem of circularity is the law of identity. The law of identity says that a thing is what a thing is, or, that a thing is what it is.

You can't argue with that. If a thing wasn't what it is, it would be something else. But, that doesn't tell us very much as in the criticism of Skinner's theory of reinforcement where he asserted that a reinforcer is reinforcing because of its effects on behavior.

To say that a reinforcer is reinforcing because it allows us to do something else or that it is reinforcing because we can then do something else may sound, to some, like saying that one behavior simply follows another. It doesn't tell us very much.

In my opinion, what saves it from being circular is that, sometimes, we do something and it hurts where hurting is something that we do. It is a behavior. In fact, it is a respondent. When that happens, we are less likely to do what made us hurt. It is punishing and not reinforcing. Not all behaviors are reinforcing.

A second argument against the criticism that the theory of reinforcement presented here is circular is that, sometimes, we do something and it doesn't allow us to do something else either now or what we have done in the past. In that case, the behavior extinguishes. It no longer occurs or we do something else in those circumstances. In other words, the principles of punishment and extinction keep the reinforcement theory presented here from being circular. Not all behaviors that follow a behavior are reinforcing.

A Disclaimer

The behavior theory presented here is not behaviorism. Behavior theory consists of the laws and principles of behavior. They are the facts of behavior and cannot be refuted. When a reinforcer follows some behavior, that behavior increases in rate. The principle of reinforcement has been demonstrated over and over again in behavior laboratories around the world. Consequently, it is considered to be a fact of behavior and not an opinion.

On the other hand, behaviorism is a philosophy of science about a science of behavior. There are those who consider it to have been refuted where to refute something means to disprove and overthrow by argument, evidence, or proof; prove to be false or erroneous.

Fortunately or unfortunately, that cannot be done with the methods of science as they are currently understood. Science is positive and not negative. It is based on proof and not disproof. It requires positive evidence and not negative evidence. Negative evidence is a lack of evidence. In other words, behaviorism cannot be refuted with the methods of science.

On the other hand, it might have been overthrown by argument or, perhaps, by consensus. The problem with logic and consensus is that logical arguments can be true according to the rules of logic but not apply anywhere in the real world. For example, if A then B, A therefore B is true according to the rules of logic but doesn't apply anywhere until we define A and B. Similarly, consensus is a matter of agreement but agreement cannot establish a matter of fact as when, for example, the consensus was that the world was flat or that the sun traveled around the earth. Wise men and women may agree when deciding life and death issues when it just ain't so as when what appears to be a corpse gets up and walks away.

Now, it may be true that behaviorism, as a philosophy of science, is dead. No one argues about it very much any more. If so, it is my opinion and only my opinion that, like the Phoenix, what has emerged from its ashes is a science of behavior. The product of that science has been presented here in the form of a behavior theory and, in particular, a behavior theory of skiing and ski teaching.

About the Author

Jay Eacker is a professor emeritus of psychology at Whitman College in Walla Walla, Washington. He holds a doctorate in general experimental psychology from Washington State University and is an alumnus level two certified ski instructor.

He has skied for over thirty years and taught skiing for about four of them at Park City Mountain Resort in Utah. Several years ago, he was voted instructor of the year by his cohorts at Ski Bluewood, a small ski resort near Dayton, Washington.